A Thousand Goodbyes

THE SURPRISING LIFE OF A FUNERAL CELEBRANT

RUTH GRAHAM

Design by Euan Monaghan
Cover illustration by Eva Polakovičová

Firstly – a big thank you for purchasing this book.
As a self-published author, it would be hugely appreciated
if you could please leave a review on Amazon: it's
the main means of getting the word out.

If you'd like to know more about me and future releases,
please follow me on Twitter: @CelebrantRuthG

* * *

Secondly: a big thank you to the families who gave permission
to share their stories. In the case of more sensitive ones,
some names and minor details have been changed.

* * *

And finally: this book has been four years in the procrastinating,
so thank also to my gifted friend and author Cat Weatherill,
for the encouragement and insightful comments that helped
me shape it all up throughout various lockdowns.

CHAPTERS

INTRODUCTION

After training to become a celebrant, it was a huge relief to discover a dedicated forum on Facebook: a private 'space' to ask questions; share and research resources; vent; and air difficulties, problems, and humorous or heart-breaking stories.

It can be very scary in the first few months with all that responsibility on your newly-trained shoulders, and it was great to see others were experiencing the same highs and lows as me, at whatever stage of their career.

I've included some of the stories from the forum in this book. They take the form of a short snippet at the end of each chapter, entitled 'A CELEBRANT SHARES'.

Reading everyone else's 'stuff' helped me put my life into perspective, and provided me with a feeling of connection. So thank you everyone for being the lovely open-minded and generous community that you are.

THE TROUBLE IS ... YOU THINK YOU HAVE TIME

Buddha

CHAPTER 1: THIS MAN HAS CEASED TO BE

Charlie Wilkins was dead.

He'd uttered his last joke; taken his last shot on the golf course; downed his final swig of brandy; and, after expelling his last breath, it was pretty certain that he'd never tell his family again that he loved them.

There was nothing more he could do. Charlie Wilkins was most definitely dead.

But yet, when the undertakers went to retrieve his body, they found him involved in some kind of bizarre family ritual, seated at a table, in front of a bowl of steaming hot soup, 'having dinner' with the rest of the family.

Apparently, it took quite a while to extricate Charlie from the scene. His family weren't keen to say goodbye. Or even to accept that he was gone.

And this continued on when I got involved, in the capacity of celebrant, employed to write and conduct his funeral service.

"We want you to talk about him as if he's still here," said his daughter, in a very determined way. "There's to be no past tense. Everything is in the present. Include him fully – and make sure you glance over to the coffin and make it a real conversation."

At the time I found that a pretty big challenge. I knew by then the family weren't dealing well with his passing, and I wasn't sure 'playing along' with the pretense that he was alive was at all a healthy thing to do.

And secondly, on a practical level, how on earth do you write a service like that and make it flow?

I like to think I've a certain amount of dexterity with words, and am able to sum up a life in a sensitive, heart-warming yet accurate way. But to do that, in a funereal environment, without acknowledging someone was actually dead, was a whole new one on me.

In the end, figuring I had no choice, I just faced it head-on, with the following words during the opening address.

'When I went to visit Charlie's wife Grace, and their daughter Lilly, they asked me to speak about Charlie in the present tense. With his big personality, and his huge laugh; those loud Hawaiian shirts, and his genuine delight for life, travel, good food, music and the people he loved, he's created too much of an impact to be just 'gone'.

'He's here amongst us now: in his children, in the unbreakable friendships he's created, and in the memories and the moments you've all shared together. So we're going to celebrate that, and include him in it all.'

And so we went on to do exactly that. Chatting about, and to Charlie, all the way through the service. And remarkably, everyone else went with it, as it seemed they didn't want to accept that he'd gone either.

It was surreal I'll admit, but it taught me that grief comes in many forms, and that people deal with death (and mortality) in their own way, in their own time.

It also taught me that the client is king, and if at all possible, you give them what they want. This is their moment, and if they want to remember someone in a particular way, a way that will allow them to move on and heal, then who are we to stop them?

Of course, on occasions refusing a request is the only option, whoever it's aimed at, whether that be the undertakers, the celebrant, the minister, or the crematorium staff.

Like the time my colleague Sheila, based at our local crem in Birmingham, was asked to put on some long white evening gloves and 'hide' at the top end of the catafalque, (the podium on which the coffin rests).

"And then," said the instructing family enthusiastically, "as the curtain closes, could you just raise your arm and give a bit of a royal wave?"

Unsurprisingly, Sheila declined the request. Not only because she'd got actual, real work to do in the office; but also, as she explained,

"I haven't got the knees for hiding behind the catafalque for thirty minutes. They must be bleedin' bonkers! And anyway," she added, "I ain't got any long, white gloves."

Having said that, I'm all for weaving a bit of humour into the service. How could I not be? I used to be a stand-up comic. But it's got to reflect the person we're talking about, and it has to be delivered well. If there's one thing ten years of treading the boards in 1980s working men's clubs has taught me – timing is everything.

I thanked my lucky stars for all that experience, when one family insisted I included the following story for their mum, (let's call her Josie), who had a knack of being in the wrong place at the wrong time.

It harked back to when Josie was in her thirties, and a keen biker. And so the story began at 'The Bulldog Bash' festival, in a queue for the unisex portaloos, where she (a tiny dot at 5 feet nothing), found herself sandwiched in the middle of a long line of men.

Now anyone who has ever been to a festival will know how hideous the toilets can be after a few days, and how long it takes to get to them when everyone's tanked up with beer and there's a rush on, but even so, after 20 minutes, still nobody had moved.

In desperation, Josie turned to the man behind her and said, "Sorry to trouble you mate. This is the queue for the toilets isn't it?"

After the biker had composed himself, he managed to say, "No love. It's not for the loos. There's a tent at the front of the line with a woman inside. She's giving out hand jobs!"

Fortunately, that got a massive roar of laughter, as everyone knew Josie and could absolutely imagine her in that situation. But I don't mind admitting, my palms were bathed in sweat before I delivered the story. You just never know who's out there listening, and how things are going to go down; but risqué or not, I think it's great that we have the opportunity to tell personal stories, and turn services into a real celebration of life.

Thirty years ago, celebrancy wasn't heard of. You got a standard send – off with hymns, prayers and readings from the bible, (or the equivalent, depending on your designated birth religion). There must be tens of thousands of people who've said goodbye to a loved one, and felt numb, angry or just lacking after a service like this, because it didn't mirror or reflect them in any way.

Thank goodness for the changes, which began in Australia, thanks to Statesman and Attorney General Lionel Murphy. He realised that secular people also wanted meaningful, personal and dignified ceremonies of substance.

It makes sense this began in a country like Australia – a country that was open to change, without thousands of years of religious dogma and tradition to overcome first. And once he'd set the wheels in motion, Murphy was proved right.

And then, celebrancy grew with a life-force that became unstoppable, spreading across the USA and throughout Europe. And just as with every living thing, it diversified along the way.

So whilst the job role of every civil or independent celebrant is the same: we all write and conduct the weddings/vow renewals/naming ceremonies and funerals that would loosely fall under the banner of 'rites of passage': how we conduct them, and the material they contain, is as different, and personal, as the people we perform them for.

In other words, every service is tailored for the individual, and to this end, we're not offended if we're asked to include religion or spirituality, or conversely, we're not upset when there isn't any. And if they want a mix of the two then that's fine as well.

This was summed up beautifully by the family who said to me, "We're not religious, but can we have The Lord's Prayer for insurance?"

And as a non-judgmental, obliging, flexible civil celebrant, I was more than happy to say, "Yes, you jolly well can."

And so throughout the book I'll introduce you to some of the quirky characters, (both dead and alive), that have been involved in these services – each and every one of them reminding me of just what an exhilarating, life affirming, poignant and sometimes hilarious job this can be.

A CELEBRANT SHARES

I feel desperately sorry for this celebrant. Sometimes there's an inkling of when things may be about to go wrong; but this is a catalogue of events you couldn't anticipate. Jackie from the Wirral's story goes like this:

* * *

'Just got back from possibly the worst funeral – EVER! Thought I'd seen it all but today stooped to the lowest level. Quite a common story: man dies aged 80: he had a second family about thirty years ago – first family incredibly bitter, second family loved him, for all his faults!

'The service was in a private chapel, organised by his current widow. Very little contact between her and his former family, so opportunity was going to be given for anyone who wanted to step up and pay tribute.

'I could see a few heads turning when I started the opening remarks, then one of the daughters stood up, made her exit, banging the door loudly on her way out. Thirty seconds later, another goes to join her.

'Into the first poem, they come back in, banging the door behind them and start talking to the others. I finish the poem and then it's time for the tributes.

'I asked by name if anyone had prepared anything – none of them had.

I then proceeded to read the wife's tribute, followed by his current mother-in-law.

'His older brother had turned up and he wanted to say something. It began with him saying they'd never got on and he'd hated him ever since he was born. He told me a little bit about their lives growing up and I tried to call it all to a halt.

'Then – and this is the killer – his brother said, 'Do you know where he was when he should have been doing his National Service? In Wormwood Scrubs – that's where he was!'

'At this point, his second family gasped – this was all news to them. I diplomatically suggested this might not be the appropriate time for bringing up old grievances – we were here to say our goodbyes in a dignified way. After a few other episodes of people storming in and out, banging doors and general shouting, I was very relieved when the final music was played.

'Afterwards, children from his original family came and spat on the coffin before they left.

'Somehow, I don't think they were intending to turn up at the wake!'

CHAPTER 2: RE-INVENTION

'How did you become a celebrant?'

I'm asked this question every week at the services I conduct. The answer is because I went to the horrendously impersonal funeral of a beautiful young friend called Jancis, who deserved more. It left me feeling angry, and her parents devastated.

It was the kind of service we've probably all encountered along the way. Full of generic offerings, where you barely recognise the person being spoken about. But in addition, this one was also delivered badly, with no sensitivity or feeling whatsoever.

Jancis was one of the sunniest, kindest and funniest people you could ever meet. We'd been founder members of the Bacardi Breezer Rapid Response Unit years ago – out drinking, dancing and up to all sorts together – as you do when you're young.

She then went on to marry twice in her short life and build a wonderful career with a chain of hair salons. In-between all this, she'd given birth to her little boy Jake, and battled several years with breast cancer. It was her love and pride in her son that kept her going, but sadly, when she finally died, Jake was still only eight years old.

There was much discussion as to whether he was old enough to attend the funeral, but in the end the decision was in favour. Traumatic though it would be, he needed closure, and something to relate to. It was felt some kind words and a bit of inclusion would do just that.

Personally, I agree. I hear too many stories of children whose parent is there one day, and gone the next, and they never seem to get past it.

A funeral answers our human need for ritual around major events, to allow us to make sense of things. And done well, this would help not only Jake, but of course, Jan's parents.

In the end, the service helped nobody. The minister conducting the funeral had been 'too busy' to spend much time with Jan's parents so what they got was a pretty standard cut and paste service, with no research behind it, and barely any personalisation.

He galloped through the introduction (which he'd obviously done thousands of times) and then when it came to the section that contained the modicum of personal detail, he constantly stumbled, calling Jancis 'Janet' twice. He said she liked Siamese cats, (she didn't – she liked Persians). And he got her age wrong.

In the end, grief-stricken though she was, Jan's mother stood up and said, "That's not what she was like. Can I just say a few words?"

Without pausing for breath, the minister replied, "No you can't. Sit down. We've got another one coming through in ten minutes."

The shock-waves ran audibly through the church. And that response will stay with Jan's mum forever. She talks about it every time I see her, and there will never be a chance to put it right. It's no exaggeration to say her healing process was stopped in its tracks that day, not to mention poor Jake's. And so, fuelled by anger, indignation and a strong desire to do better for people, that's how the idea of becoming a celebrant took root.

At this juncture, I have to say, not every minister does a bad job (of course they don't). And not every celebrant does a great job. As in all things, there is light and shade and degrees of professionalism and conscience.

But most celebrants are drawn to the job because we want to make a difference, and we're prepared to spend the time with families to create services that allow people able to heal: or in the case of a wedding, to celebrate in a really unique way that wouldn't be allowed in a church or registry office.

For funerals, we put in the hours with the families to learn about the deceased properly, and spend hours writing up the notes at the other end. This enables us to deliver a really quality service when the day comes.

And I have to admit, what also appealed to me was the unique combination of no fixed routine (anathema to me); plus people contact, and the knowledge that I may finally be doing a useful job with real purpose and meaning.

I've always struggled with this. Not cut out in any way for a general nine-to-five, it's been a long road to finding the right career. A very long road. Forty years in fact!

Those years have seen my endeavours in stand-up comedy: battling to be heard in working men's clubs from Glasgow to Newcastle; dealing with hecklers like the one from Swansea Dockers' Club who said; "Get off you're crap. Or tell us a joke we know!"

The graft continued on through my ill-fated appearance on New Faces (hosted by the lovely Marti Caine) – where Nina Myscow described me as 'Fat, short and unfunny.'

Disillusioned with showbiz for a while, I then changed tack, moving into sales: first in advertising space, and then on to carphones in the very, very early days. Back when they were so heavy, carrying them around would give you instant biceps.

When I began working for FCA Telecom (Forest Car Audio), there were just three transmitters in the whole country. Getting the phones to work was a challenge, and I wasn't at all convinced about their potential.

This contributed to my visible lack of enthusiasm – a direct contrast to my colleague Zed's approach. Somehow, Zed managed to make a sale every time he left the building, and clients loved him.

When asked to provide a testimonial for the next sales brochure, one local wide boy wrote; 'Thank you Zed. Next to my cock, that phone you flogged me is the most useful tool I've ever owned.'

I'm not sure that feedback ever got used: just as my approach to selling never found its way into the training manual. Bored and unchallenged, the final straw was when my boss overheard my response to a telephone enquiry. On being asked how much the phones started at, I responded:

"Well sir, the in-car version starts at £750 fully-fitted" – (an *enormous* amount of money for a phone, back in the mid-1980s).

After recovering his composure, the client then said, "£750! I thought they'd start at around £250?"

To which I replied, "Ooh sorry no. For that, we could probably only fit you a loud hailer on your roof rack."

More jobs then followed: tv walk-on work; acting; secretarial temping; hospitality on cruise liners; song writing and then on to teaching English in a young offenders' prison.

I thought I'd found my vocation there until, due to cutbacks, the guards were removed from the landing and we were issued with walkie-talkies instead.

The little sods in the classroom spotted this weakness in the system, and one day, Valentine (handsome, nineteen, in for raping an old lady and ripping her heart out), announced, "Do you realise miss? We could all have you, and nobody would know until break-time."

This horrifying statement, combined with a dumpling palmed to me from the kitchen staff, containing a note threatening the same fate; was enough to send me on my way.

The mercurial career gods then saw me enter the less-hazardous but equally cut-throat world of journalism and publishing; and then more recently, in a move that nobody has ever managed to fathom; I ended up playing fiddle in an Irish party band called Celtic Clan.

What I'm trying to demonstrate from this list, whether you see it as risible, fanciful, joyful, experimental, lost or brave; is that it's shown me 'life'. And somehow, all this stuff, and all those experiences have come together in the end, to allow me to really understand its challenges, and peoples' quirks. I truly feel qualified to do the job well.

So now, I sit in living rooms with families, posthumously getting to know their loved ones. I deftly avoid being drawn into family politics, even as they unfold around me. I drink tea and coffee of varying qualities, stroke pets, make small talk, comfort people and get them to the stage where they're relaxed enough to laugh, cry, argue, disagree and support each other, even with a stranger in their midst.

I ask questions and scribble notes madly as the life stories, (sometimes mundane but more often than not, quite incredible), reveal themselves. And then, I go away to craft something inspiring that will celebrate the person's life and reflect their and their family's wishes.

It's a minefield, requiring so very many different skills. The subject matter ensures it's not the job for everyone, but it's certainly broadened my horizons, and I love it.

And when all the late-night writing, difficult family visits and stress get a bit much, all I have to do is remember one particular story from the showbiz years to get perspective:

It was back in 1987 when I was a new stand-up. I was young and naïve at the time, so when my agent sent me to support a 'household name' at the Villa Marina in the Isle of Man, I just took the gig. It didn't even occur to me to ask who the household name actually was.

All I could see in my mind's eye was me going out to this glamorous venue, and knocking everyone for six with my comedy and my Coronation Street and Hi-de-Hi impressions.

That image soon changed on arrival, when I realised the Isle of Man had been taken over by bikers for the island's very first TT races, and the name I was supporting was actually the extremely un-PC comic Bernard Manning.

The reality turned out to be even worse than the realisation. When the show began, it was literally everything I was dreading, and so much more.

The first act was a lovely young girl called Giselle, who sang beautifully and oozed sex appeal. The bikers loved her – no problem.

She was followed by a stripper called Pearl Barley, who worked with a live snake. At one stage, Pearl even removed her jewel-encrusted bra, to 'weigh' the snake in one of its humongous cups. The snake nestled in there nicely, to roars of approval from the bikers.

And then there was me.

Full of fear I over-compensated; bursting on to the stage with the opening song, 'I Was Born With A Smile On My Face,' (by Stephanie de Sykes).

I trilled away for dear life, but the bikers weren't impressed. Nor did they like my Hi-de-Hi impressions, (no chance of a 'Ho-de-Ho' response from any of them). By the time I'd got around to doing Shirley Bassey, they were positively in uproar.

Then the first lager can hit me, full in the face. That was the cue for everyone else to follow suit, and from then on it was mayhem, as a shower of metal rained down.

After twenty minutes, I was clanking around the stage like the Tin Man from The Wizard of Oz, wondering whether I should just call it, and my career, a day.

Suddenly, there was a roar from the bikers. I turned to look behind, and saw Bernard Manning bursting through the rear curtains, charging towards me. Plainly, he couldn't bear it either.

Bernard grabbed the microphone out of my hand and in his trademark gruff voice appealed to the crowd saying: 'Come on lads. Calm down. Give the poor cow a chance!'

They didn't.

But the lifeline he'd thrown me, (and the desire not to lose my fee), gave me the courage to plough on to the end of my forty-five minute spot.

When I finished, I made my way backstage, to find Bernard waiting in the wings. Immediately I spotted him I said, "Thank you so, so much Mr Manning."

To which he responded, "That's alright love. S'pose there's no chance of a shag?"

On seeing the shock upon my face, Bernard followed up very quickly with, "I'll take that as a no then. Why? Is it something I said?"

Looking back, it's quite funny. But remembering the story still serves its purpose. Would I rather be in front of two thousand baying bikers? Or a few hundred mourners, who, sad though it all is, actually want to hear what I'm saying?

And once again, perspective and enthusiasm are renewed.

A CELEBRANT SHARES

This one from Robbie in Canada made me howl:

* * *

'As a bagpiper, I play many gigs. Recently I was asked by a funeral director to play at a graveside service for a homeless man. He had no family or friends, so the service was to be at a pauper's cemetery in the Nova Scotia back country.

'Unfortunately, I wasn't familiar with the backwoods. I got lost and being a typical man; didn't stop to ask for directions.

'I finally arrived an hour late. The hearse was nowhere in sight and it was evident the funeral guys had gone. There were only the diggers and crew left and they were eating lunch. Even so, I felt badly and apologised to the men for being late.

'I went to the side of the grave and looked down and the vault lid was already in place. I didn't know what else to do, so I started to play.

'The workers put down their lunches and began to gather around. I played out my heart and soul for this man with no family and friends. I played like I've never played before for this homeless man.

'And as I played 'Amazing Grace', the workers began to weep. They wept; I wept; we all wept together. When I finished, I packed up my bagpipes and started for my car. Though my head was hung low, my heart was full.

'As I opened the door to my car, I heard one of the workers say, "Wow. In all my years of putting in septic tanks, I've never seen anything like that before!"'

CHAPTER 3: FOREWARNED IS FORE-ARMED

When I take instructions for a job, it's usually over the phone from a funeral director (FD). As part of the chat, the FD will let me know about any family issues, disagreements or unusual circumstances. This was the case with Alan, who was described to me as 'Absolutely lovely, but a bit prone to over-enthusiasm. In fact, I think he's on a spectrum of some kind.'

Never one to shy away from a challenge, I thanked the FD for the heads-up, and after my initial call, (in which Alan sounded very, er, let's call it 'buoyant'), I went along to meet him in person.

I met Alan at a restaurant in a farm shop. It was the perfect combination of halfway between the two of us. Lively enough to provide a backdrop for meeting a stranger, without being so noisy that I'd find it impossible to write.

After the introductions (Call me Al. I won't bite – ha,ha!), we ordered coffee, I got out my notepad and the story began. I heard about his mum Jean: a sporty, lively lady who loved to partake and watch. She took up marathon running in her forties, and travelled solo across India in her seventies.

She did meals on wheels for the 'old' people, (until her co-pilot and friend pointed out that they were both older and in worse condition than the people they were helping). What a character – I was going to enjoy getting to know Jean through her son.

I heard of how she'd encouraged him to take his eleven-plus early, and how she'd stood on the touchline of a football game, cheering him on.

And then suddenly, without warning, Al said, "Did I mention she used to whip me with a wet towel?"

I baulked. Where did on earth had that come from?

"Ah!" I retorted, "But that was in the days when it was okay to hit your kids wasn't it? Ha, ha ..." I trailed off, nervously.

"But it wasn't OK," he responded, slightly glassy-eyed as he stroked his side, comforting the long-gone wounds.

"And my dad. Did I mention the football game when I scored from a penalty, and all he could say was how well the team played? Nothing about me at all?"

And that was it. With no further warning, we were off on a self-pity mini-break.

I kept trying to drag Al back, distracting him with questions.

What about your mum's friends – she sounded very popular. What would they say about her? And travel? Yes; more travel stories please! Was she religious at all? What were her thoughts on God, or spirituality?

He answered all my questions in some fashion or another, but somehow managed to fit in all his own stories of disappointment or loss, finishing with how getting to grammar school had spoilt his life.

"But why?" I asked. "Surely going there had steered you in a really positive direction?"

"But it wasn't the right one Ruth," he said, visibly welling up as he spoke. "I wanted to be an actor, but was never listened to."

I could empathise with all this to be honest. My own mother; (a terrifying northern hybrid of Thora Hird, Hilda Baker and Hyacinth Bucket), had been less than nurturing or encouraging to my own dreams of treading the boards. (I still remember the line 'I'm not taking on a second job to support your ridiculous ideas.')

I could see in Al the same signs of low self-esteem that I'd struggled with for years, and was just about to trot out a platitude or two when he, (bearing in mind we're in a farm shop café), leapt to his feet and thumped the table *really* hard.

Al paused for dramatic effect. Then, looking around to check whose attention he'd caught, he yelled, "Fuck it! FUCK IT!!!! I've still got Lear in me!!!"

I can't tell you how I handled it. I must have blacked out for a few seconds with horror. All I can recall is a sea of stunned, frozen faces. A lady choked quietly on her tea. Spoons clattered down upon saucers. Shocked silence enveloped the room. It was truly, truly awful.

I brought the meeting to an abrupt halt after that. But not before Al had managed to thrust at me a list of nine (honestly) of his mum's friends to call for 'more anecdotes'.

Thanks to those nine calls, and continual emails from Al, the service took several days to compile. And bless 'em – most of Jean's old friends all said the same thing, about her being 'lovely' and 'a bit of a character'. By call number six I knew what was coming, but you know what it's like with older people: they'd been promised a call, so a call they had to have.

Finally, I collated all the information, put together the service wording and sent it for approval. To Al's credit, he did respond that he loved what I'd written and was having a little weep at home as he read it.

On the actual day of the service, Al turned up in a baggy, cream linen suit, (the kind of thing you'd wear in the searing heat of Singapore in the days of the old Empire). Rather incongruously, he'd teamed the suit with a pair of chainmail-effect shoes with individual toes in. They're called 'Five Fingers Barefoot Running Shoes': ('Feel The World Beneath You'). It was a look, I'll grant you that.

So up he strolled to the crematorium door, with his partner by his side. On spotting me in my black dress and boots, Al wolf-whistled loudly, whilst miming an hourglass shape with his hands.

"Mmmm," he bellowed. "Check *you* out!"

Rather mortifyingly, everybody then turned to do just that. I felt the embarrassment burning up from the soles of my feet. It tends to do that with me: embarrassment is warm and works up me vertically; while shock and fear are cold, and shoot downwards.

This occasion prompted a burning rush that took in every organ from the heart to the pit of the stomach, ending in a grand finale of jelly knees.

I tried to bat such indiscretion off with a non-committal and fairly standard, "Good morning. How are you?"

I then turned to the lady, and with my friendliest smile to dilute the collateral damage said, "Hello. I'm Ruth. You must be Al's partner?"

To her credit, she did smile and say hello, but it wasn't the best start. Nor was leading the coffin into the crem, usual ceremonial pace applied, only to be stopped in my tracks by Al's searingly-loud whistle. This time, it was the kind you'd use on a sheep dog; followed by the words, 'Oi, Ruth! Come back and start again. Beryl's behind you on the zimmer, and she can't keep up!'

I turned to see Beryl, (who was one of the ladies I'd called for anecdotes), edging along at the speed of an arthritic snail in a salt mine. Somehow, she'd managed to place herself behind me, but in front of the coffin, and was holding up the entire proceedings.

I went back to the door to start again. Beryl was shifted to the side, and in we all went, at varying speeds, to the strains of the 'Goodness Gracious Me': a very un-PC homage to Jean's travels around India.

The service then proceeded relatively well, although I did have to cope with the fact that Al was surreptitiously taking photos of me from under his jacket.

But, ever the professional, I ploughed on; mentally writing it off as part of his 'quirkiness'; (although with the outbursts, the odd clothing and the indiscretion with the camera, I'm still not entirely sure what 'spectrum' he was actually on).

But I did get a lovely email a few days later, when the embarrassment and general disquiet about Al had settled. I was actually rather touched by his missive, telling me he'd had chance to reflect on the day, and how my words had allowed him to put mum's memory into a warmer place in his heart.

And as a thank you, he'd attached a couple of the clandestine photos he'd taken of me. Despite them being blurry, out of focus and at the most unflattering angle you can imagine, they came with an invitation to 'Feel free to use these on your website.'

I looked at them again and had to laugh. Al had taken them from such a low angle that he'd created not a double, but a triple chin. Teamed with a softened face, no discernible jawline and creases of fat over the collar of my blouse, he'd managed to make me look just like just like a frill-necked lizard.

But I emailed Al back and thanked him for his kind thought, whilst pondering on how there really is now't so queer as folk.

So, contrast this story of ebullient over-sharing and enthusiasm, with the story of Kerys, who couldn't have been less keen to engage with me, speak to me or even look in my direction when I went to meet her family.

I turned up at the house at the allotted time, with an expectation of meeting the widow and her daughter. When I rang the bell, the door flew open seconds later, to reveal a middle-aged woman and a very enthusiastic Labrador, that launched itself immediately at my privates.

"Come on in – it's the dog's birthday," she said, making no attempt to pull the dog away. There was also no introduction, no 'Hello I'm x', so I had no clue if it was mother or daughter at this stage.

When I entered the room, to my surprise there were four more people in there. A couple of them said hello; two of them ignored me, and still, nobody introduced themselves.

Eventually, I sussed out there was the widow Jenny and her daughter Kerys; plus Kerys' nameless boyfriend, and two other women (one of whom had answered the door). These were the deceased's daughters, from his first marriage.

The atmosphere was cordial, but it wasn't comfortable by any means. There were plainly issues between the first daughters and

Kerys, and as I watched everyone treading on eggshells, it was obviously who ruled the roost.

It was also obvious Kerys was not happy that I was in the room; and for the first ten minutes, she refused to even acknowledge me. Both she and her boyfriend, (whose name I never did discover), just stared at the wall, somehow managing to simultaneously emit hostile vibes in my direction.

I concentrated on the mum and two older sisters, doing what I usually do: asking questions, probing a little deeper in-between the top layers of what they were offering, trying to tease out a fuller picture.

It was hard graft, as the deceased, Kevin, had led a good, but not particularly interesting life: one job, rising up the ranks in plastic mouldings: not a fan of holidays, his favourite saying had been,

'Why go abroad when it's all here?'

He also didn't drive; and had a very small set of friends. You get the picture …

But when I asked what he was like as a father, the touchpaper was lit. Kerys flew up from the sofa, exiting through the double doors. I swear her feet barely touched the carpet!

I ploughed on with the remaining sisters: special memories of childhood? Anything he'd done or said that particularly encouraged you to go in one direction or the other? Was he kind or strict? Humorous perhaps? (No bloody chance, but I had to ask!)

When we got to the anecdote about how he used to help Kerys with her homework, she flew back in through the door.

"Don't tell my stories! And I'd rather that wasn't mentioned anyway!"

Then she turned to glare at me, making furious eye-contact at last.

"I find it reprehensible that you're a stranger in our home, listening to all this. And then you're going to pretend that you knew my dad. It's just wrong."

I took a deep breath.

I explained that wasn't my intention at all and that in an ideal world, every family would conduct their own services. What could be more personal? But in the event they don't feel strong enough or able to compile and conduct a service, then they need a third party.

I ended on the line, "So really Kerys, I'm a conduit for the family. I'm simply there to help you all express what you'd like to say, and help you put it all together."

She didn't look at all convinced, and although she did speak to me a little after that, it was begrudgingly. But for me, the worst part was how she completely vetoed everything her sisters said; riding rough-shod all over them.

Every time they offered up a memory or a suggestion, it was shot down. She corrected her mother; contradicted and challenged every-thing and was thoroughly unpleasant. It's the first time I've actively disliked someone whilst in this role.

To be honest, her attitude not only annoyed me, it really quite upset me. I'd not encountered such hostility before, or such unfair-ness. I wasn't given a chance to make any kind of impression before she decided how much to like or dislike me. It was a fait accompli before I walked in; and like I say, absolutely unfair.

After fretting about it all evening, I then decided to call the FD the next day to tell them. Just in case there was any bad feedback, I wanted to get my pennyworth in there first.

Once that was off my chest, I got on with the writing; but it was done with a heavy heart. I sent it back to the family for approval, (fat chance!), and tried to put it to the back of my mind whilst I went on holiday to Portugal.

Even there; amongst the beauty of the Algarve, and the humour of the menu translations ('Try our wines. They leave you nothing to hope for!'); I couldn't let it go. It's no exaggeration to say that Kerys ruined my first holiday in years; and of course the minute we landed, she was fully back on my mind. I was dreading her feedback on my script for the service.

And sure enough, the draft had come back with monumental changes, elevating Kevin from caring but plodding dad to almost saint-like status; while almost erasing the first daughters from history.

This rose-tinted perspective always makes me smile. Along the way I've seen some cracking alterations and euphemisms.

For example, if someone's had an affair, it's often couched as them having an 'irresistible attraction'.

If mum/daughter didn't get on, it's usually covered by the phrase, 'All mother daughter relationships are difficult at times; but as Josephine mellowed, she and her daughter found several common interests.'

If a father wasn't open and loving, us celebrants will hear something like, 'Dad wasn't of the generation that showed emotion openly: he showed his love through practical means, by working hard and providing.'

This script was no exception. A particularly inventive example of Kerys' editing was the following: my original wording had said, 'After failing his first driving test, Kevin never took another. He was a hard taskmaster, and as he didn't like to achieve anything less than perfection, he chose not to subject himself to another attempt'.

Kerys had changed this to: 'Kevin was always healthy and fit. And part of that regime included never driving but preferring to walk everywhere. He especially enjoyed walking to work every day through the park, taking in the beauty of the nature and birdsong.'

So, even though I know the real situation, if that's what the family want to hear, and it makes them feel better, then so be it. It's not my job to preach, or argue with a family of strangers about the accuracy of the eulogy. And in this particular case, I was just happy it had all been dealt with.

On the day of the service however, the silent treatment continued. I'd hoped things would thaw a little, but as soon as the front doors of the chapel were opened I saw there was no chance.

I tried to make eye contact with the family. Kerys and her mum were stood by the hearse, but made no attempt to say hello. They looked at the coffin, the other mourners and the floor – anything but me.

I kept on trying; actually over-trying, thinking 'surely they'll crack eventually'. I was almost ridiculous at this stage, feeling like a table-spoon of pureed turnip, being danced around in front of a reluctant toddler's mouth. But no – they weren't going for it.

I felt sick inside. Celebrancy is a demanding enough role, without the additional pressure of knowing the clients don't like you. I tried one more time, but was again met with a blank, so in the end I turned my back, nodded to the bearers, and in we went.

Kerys and her mum took up their seats at the front. The other daughters were relegated to three rows back. I began speaking, but it felt like a very dry service. No hymns or prayers as he wasn't religious. No poetry ('he wasn't like that'). No funny anecdotes, and no music to listen to in the middle (he wasn't 'like that' either, apparently). The irony was, they'd booked a double slot at the crem; and there was so little content it was, in the true sense of the word, almost pathetic.

I watched Kerys and her mum, still avoiding any eye-contact; but they were obviously not happy with something. The delivery perhaps? It couldn't be the content, as they'd fine tooth-combed it already.

They were shuffling around, whispering and oscillating between looking stony-faced, or irritated or bored. Then suddenly, the mum looked up, pointed at her daughter and mouthed, 'HER READING', in the exaggerated way that people do when they're trying to make a point.

I nodded. The reading was coming up. I couldn't wait for the bloody reading; for it to come up, be done with; and for it all to be over. For good!

I introduced Kerys, who approached, still managing to avoid eye contact. She stood on the podium, and delivered a few words, with absolutely no substance to them. If you're going to tell people 'I have so many happy memories of dad', then share a few, for God's sake. Brighten it all up. Turn him from the one-dimensional character you've portrayed him as to me, into someone with a bit of life and colour. But no; she droned on, telling us nothing in five hundred words.

By the time it was over, I was literally drenched in sweat. Standing outside greeting the mourners, I can't tell you how grateful I was for a bit of fresh air. But first I had to deal with Kerys, who lead the mourners on the way out.

Of course, out of manners and professionalism, I acknowledged her. "Thanks Kerys."

She sniffed, made full, hard eye-contact with me for the first time, and just stalked straight past. Her mum never said a word either.

I spoke to Sam the FD when he came out of the chapel after the final mourner. He told me he'd had a taste of her charming approach too. Apparently, at the very beginning of the funeral, when everyone was still waiting outside, he'd gone over to give the instructions, saying, "Ladies. The bearers will take up the coffin, and then if you'd just like to follow on after ..." That was as far as he'd got, before being corrected by Kerys, who said, "It's not a coffin, it's a box."

Like I'd done so many times in my dealings with her, apparently he'd just taken a deep breath, and said, "As you wish madam," before she interrupted him again.

This time it was a complaint about the flowers. Sam said, "Did we do them?" To which she responded, "No, but ..."

Sam cut her off in her stride, flattening his hands in a conciliatory gesture that also said 'enough now', followed by the words, "Like I said madam. This way. After the coffin ..."

Yes, I understand she was upset. Her apparently healthy father of seventy six had dropped dead with no warning. But other people we see are upset too. Their loved-one went to work and didn't come home; or battled a horrendous illness, with all the devastation that brings to the wider family. But still they manage to treat us politely when we go to visit.

Sam and I ended that morning in agreement that there's grief, and there's manners; and the two of them aren't mutually exclusive.

A CELEBRANT SHARES

Angela in Wigan says:

* * *

'Oh my God! This is a first. I've just been to see a family, and come home only to realise my wallet is missing from my bag! I've searched the car, and I know I didn't leave it at home.

'I can't help thinking that someone pinched it when I was in their bathroom.

'How on earth am I going to face the family on the day?'

CHAPTER 4: SAFETY IN NUMBERS

When estate agent Stephanie Slater disappeared whilst at work in 1992, it sparked a national manhunt. Thankfully, she was discovered eight days later, although having been crammed into a wheelie bin/ makeshift coffin, and repeatedly raped, she wasn't in a good way.

Her abduction by Michael Sams, highlighted the question of how women stay safe in situations when they're alone with strangers; especially in isolated places.

Stephanie had been showing Sams around a potential property. There were no members of the public around to hear her shouts or come to her aid. And since doing this job, it's occurred to me more than once how vulnerable I am too.

I live alone; have no close family, and no set routine. If I was to go missing, nobody would actually notice for several days: (and even then, they'd probably just think I was out having fun). Once I've taken instruction to do the job, the FD doesn't get involved again. As far as they're concerned I'm at home, writing up the service, and they'll see me on the day of the funeral.

It's not a feeling that makes me terribly secure, especially after the visit to Del in my early days of celebrancy.

If I'm honest, Del didn't seem 'right' on the phone. And the fact he was ringing me direct, having found me off the internet should definitely have sounded alarms. But I was naïve back then. I didn't realise I should have referred him back to his chosen FD, so they could check all the details out and then formally instruct me to visit him.

Instead, reasoning I was skint and couldn't be turning down work on a whim, (and with the understanding that everyone's map of the world is different), I booked an appointment to meet Del and chat about his deceased mum.

It was an evening appointment: he couldn't make the day as he had to be 'available for the job centre', so I duly turned up around 7pm, just as the light was fading.

It was a rough estate and the flat was hard to find; but I didn't want to ask directions from any of the kids lurking around. They looked crisp-fed and feral; the sort of kids who'd regard a women with a clipboard and writing pad as a bit of good sport. Or a meal for the muscular Staffie dogs that most of them were hanging out with.

I eventually found Del's flat. It had a side door, which led up a set of uncarpeted wooden stairs. I heard Del bounding down them. When he opened the door, I was quite surprised to see a huge Rasta with gold teeth beaming at me. He was wearing a vest, shorts and flip flops, and was sweating profusely.

"Come on in man. Excuse the state of me crib. I'm laying floorboards."

I followed him up: (advice now given to estate agents; never go up first as you can be grabbed from behind); and we entered into a small lounge with half the floorboards missing.

It was a random arrangement, (think two down here; five up there; one down here and there); with nowhere discernibly large enough to place a chair. The only patch in the whole room that had any stretch of usable flooring was underneath the piano, so that's where we ended up, sitting around it as if it was a table.

Del offered me a drink, and seemed puzzled when I declined.

"What? You think I'm gonna lace it?"

"Blimey no. Ha, ha. God forbid! I'm just not thirsty, thank you Del."

"As long as you sure ..."

He eyed me suspiciously, jabbing at a couple of piano keys for good measure. Anger in B flat.

Not the best start, but I got out my pad, gently leaned it on the ivories and started asking questions. I was on an old piano stool. Del was seated directly next to me; but much higher, on a kitchen barstool.

I could smell his breath on top of me, but even more disconcertingly – I could see right up the leg of his shorts. I had a horrible feeling this was by design, as he'd very visibly gone commando. And that was when the first prickle of fear started to stir.

Del wasn't the best interviewee ever. Not only was he fairly abrupt in his answers, they didn't seem to have any relevance to what I was asking.

"Were you close to your mum Del?"

"She made good jerk chicken."

"Oh, that's nice. What about brothers or sisters? Did she have any family?" (I was still acting normal at this stage. Steady voice. Pen poised. Eye contact, but nothing challenging).

"One of them's a lesbian in the Caribbean. She's not coming to the funeral."

"Ah, O.K. Yes. Probably a bit far?"

"What? Are you saying she not worth it?"

Oh God I thought, he's misreading me now. At this stage my heart started to beat a bit faster

"No, of course not. Just, if they're older relatives, it's a long way to travel." (Quick – change the subject) – "What about hobbies? What did she enjoy doing?"

Del's eyes took on a misty glaze then. "She loved 'dis. Dis piano," he gestured. "Do you play?"

"Me? No, ha ha. I play violin and guitar and sing a bit, but no; not the piano."

His eyes lit up then. "You sing? Ah! I've bin lookin' for someone to sing with!"

Without hesitation, Del leapt off his stool and began to play. It was a little halting and stiff; he was no Elton John; but I did recognise the strains of 'Endless Love'. Then Del began to croon the part of Lionel Richie.

"Two hearts, two hearts that beat as one. Our love has just begun."

He turned to me enthusiastically. "It sound better with a Reggae feel, yeah?"

"Lovely," I beamed back. "Really good. But can we talk about your mum?"

He ignored me, taken with the music now. "Come on. You be Diana Ross."

I've been in some situations in my time, but this one left me flummoxed. It was funny, in a way. But I couldn't read Del at all. The mood change, the sudden enthusiasm, the lack of underwear. I was actually scared not to be Diana right then, so I joined in.

As we ploughed on through the verses, Del promising he wanted to share all his love with me 'as no-one else will do'.

Around the time we were pledging that our two hearts would beat as one, I split off into a harmony, which Del seemed really pleased with. Eventually, we climaxed with, "No-one can deny. This love I have inside."

"I'll give it all to you," swore Del

"My love."

(Together) "My, endless love..."

It petered out to a silence. The atmosphere hung heavy between us.

It was a bit like waking up in the morning realising you've had sex with someone you don't fancy. But you've done it anyway, and now you don't know how to get out.

And I'd done it. I'd duetted, (in harmony!), with a stranger with no pants on.

But fortunately, Del saved the day. With no preamble whatsoever, he simply flicked a mental switch and said,

"She ain't 'avin no funeral."

"Sorry? Doreen – your mum? What do you mean Del?"

"I ain't payin'. The council can do it."

"Okaaay. So what do you mean? You don't want it to happen at all? Or it's not happening now? Or you want to think about it?"

The last idea seemed to appeal. "Yeah. I'm gonna think."

He paused for a few seconds, before adding, almost childlike, "Thanks for coming. I'll let you know."

I've heard those words, 'I'll let you know', a thousand times at auditions throughout the years. Now I was hearing it from a delusional man who, for all I knew, didn't even have a dead mother. But the difference was, this time I was more than happy to be 'let go'.

Somehow, I managed to grab my pad, navigate the patchy flooring, and be at the door before Del had stood up and re-arranged his testicles.

It wasn't until I was in the car, with the doors locked and the engine turning over, that I allowed myself to laugh: really loudly, almost hysterically.

The real, gut-wrenching realisation at what a close shave I'd had, would come later.

But you know, I'm not the only one to get caught out in the heat of the moment. My colleague Jen found herself in a horrendous situation when she went to visit a middle-aged couple mourning the death of the much-loved matriarch of the family.

At first glance it all seemed very innocuous. A nice home in a nice middle-class area. A warm welcome from them both, and lots of lovely stories at the ready to keep the conversation flowing.

And then it happened. The wife went off to make a drink, and without a moment's notice, the husband launched himself across the room and stuck his hand straight up Jen's skirt! No conversation; no eye contact and no warning.

She reported later how it all felt as if it was happening in slow-motion. Of how the incongruity of it left her at once frozen with horror, but somehow still able to work out how to play things.

In the few seconds it took, she calculated that if she screamed, it would cause a huge panic. And if she got up and went, the wife would, similarly, be left confused and upset – wondering what on earth had happened. And bless her, lovely Jen didn't want to cause the lady any more anguish.

But matters were taken out of her hands when the wife walked in, just as husband was withdrawing his hand from Jen's skirt. She'd only come to ask if Jen took sugar, but as you can imagine, the words froze on her lips.

It all kicked off from there, and in-between the wife's screeching, and launching herself at Jen, my unfortunate friend managed to reach the door and get out of the house. Upon reflection, she just felt terrible about the whole situation, which is totally wrong, because she most certainly wasn't at fault.

God knows what happened in the house after she'd gone. I can only imagine. I know Jen had some explaining to do to the FD, but ultimately she was relieved not to have to do the service.

I believe the task then fell to a male vicar, which, given the circumstances, was probably for the best.

A CELEBRANT SHARES

This story is from a celebrant in Sussex, who had only been doing the job for two weeks at the time:

* * *

'I've just been to meet a family. Quite a heady cocktail going on in the living room. I had to get the story against the backdrop of nineteen parakeets squawking, a Great Dane trying to sit on my lap, and the son smoking cannabis in the room next door.

'Well – I did say I wanted variety in my new career!'

CHAPTER 5: WORDS ARE ALL I HAVE

I received an email once. It said:

'Dear Ruth. We cannot thank you enough for what you did for us at dad's service. Your words managed to combine the enormity of goodbye, whilst giving us hope for the future.'

I've never forgotten that email. It was a reminder of the responsibility we carry for every family. How it's vital to get it right each and every time. If we don't, the alternative is a service like my friend Jancis had, leaving a family with the opposite of hope for the future.

Finding the right words for any occasion takes thought, research and time. A love of language helps too – something inherent in me; but sadly, not nurtured in my early years.

Raised on 'Janet and John' books, I progressed on to Enid Blyton, and then inexplicably, things stopped. After this level there were no more books around the home. It seemed I could read, had an average vocabulary, and that was deemed enough to get by.

As a result, I remember being desperate to get to school, to escape and lose myself in the library at break time. Finding new words, working out their meanings, was a joy. And when I'd unearthed some new ones, I'd lie awake at night, practicing them in different scenarios and sentences – afraid they'd be lost overnight if they weren't deeply embedded.

I raced through the library contents, particularly excited by the 'Shirley Flight, Air Hostess' series. After these; I was despairing of what to read next, when my friend Luella Keeley produced a James Bond novel from her satchel.

"It's dad's," she whispered. "He won't miss it if you read it quickly."

That meant taking it home, where I'd barely got past the first chapter, before mum found it. She went ballistic.

Her initial argument was that the subject-matter was 'too advanced' for me. I retorted that I was ten years old, we'd all been doing sex education for two years, and besides – I'd just learnt the word 'fellatio' from Melissa Keogh.

I thought she was actually going to pass out.

Her second argument, which actually rang truer, was, 'People like us don't need long words. Stick with what you know.'

That sentence sums up the backdrop of mediocrity and indifference against which I was raised. Don't rock the boat. Don't question. Don't stand out.

There was little chance of that. I was plain and mousy; I wore second-hand clothes before 'pre-loved' had ever been heard of; and my friend's mum had already told her she wasn't to hang out with me because I was 'common'. No surprise I had no confidence that I was any good at anything; and this carried through into senior school.

Thankfully, this changed with the arrival of a new teacher – Mr May. It was the mid-1970s. He was handsome and dapper; with sparkling, kind eyes and full of an enthusiasm I'd not encountered in anyone before, delighting in people; his work and life in general.

Mr May taught drama. And although I could never attend his day or after-school classes, I did have access to him occasionally when he stood in for the English teachers.

I remember clearly in his second lesson with us; we were asked to write a two-page introduction to ourselves. We could choose the first or the third person. I didn't know what that meant, and was too shy to ask, but spotting me looking around nervously, Mr May slid over when everyone else was writing.

Within a minute, thanks to his crystal-clear explanation, I was off, and he shot me a fabulous smile when he saw the penny had dropped.

To begin, I didn't feel I'd got much to say, so I centred the story around my job as a waitress at Bracebridge Café in our local park; and the conversations I'd overheard.

When I got the piece back with his comments, it simply said, 'You, missy, are a writer.'

I could have wept. His words gave *me* hope for the future.

And just to ensure I stayed on the ball; Mr May regularly came up with book suggestions: on subjects as diverse as Zen meditation, through to Scoop by Evelyn Waugh; (and most obligingly, he'd get them ordered into the library so I didn't have to pay).

He also set me and a few other 'rescued' students some unofficial challenges, like debates, which he'd referee in his spare time. These encouraged us to develop our critical thinking skills, and how to unpick another's argument: all whilst he shouted from the sidelines; "No! Find a stronger word than stubborn. Recalcitrant! Yes – good, good ..."

He was probably in the last generation of teachers that was allowed to teach creatively and with freedom. There were fewer restrictions in the 1970s. Less paperwork to do and not such rigid guidelines. And if you skipped PE to go to a debate – who cared?

Mr May's input made my life so much happier. He ignited ambition in me; the antithesis of all the negativity and restrictions at home. He reinforced the beauty and the *power* of language: tools that can open so many doors. It was such a crying shame that I was ill for the last two weeks of the final term. That I never got to say goodbye to him. To thank him for literally changing the course of my life.

I never forgot Mr May.

Over the next few years at secretarial college, and on through the wretched world of office temping, I frequently wondered how things had turned out for him.

I got the answer decades later in 2019, when I took instructions for his funeral.

At first, when the FD said the name 'Brian May', I thought he was talking about the guitarist in Queen. Then common sense struck. To my knowledge, Brian May the guitarist didn't live in Sutton Coldfield. It had to be someone else.

It wasn't until I met his wife Pat, and started hearing the stories, that I realised it was *my* Mr May! When the realisation dawned, it was a good job I was sitting down.

And so the stories unfolded; of how Brian had been a student at Cambridge, and won the prize for Actor of The Year. The Cambridge News extolled his virtues, and the breadth of his leading roles, from Lear to Waiting for Godot.

I heard of how he'd met Pat, the love of his life as a student, going on to marry her when they were just twenty two years old.

And how, shortly after the arrival of their first baby, Brian had received a phone call at 10.30 one evening. It was from *the* Melvyn Bragg no less: offering Brian his own TV chat show!

Incredibly, he turned it down, as they'd just started a family and Brian wanted to devote himself to that. What an amazing sacrifice for a man with such talent.

But TV's loss was the education system's gain, and Brian spent the next forty years inspiring students. Even out of work time he was devoted to what he did. He took older students to the pub for script read-throughs. He took others carol singing at Christmas to help them overcome shyness.

And I've no doubt the generations after me were treated with exactly the same enthusiasm and love that I'd been shown.

His wife told me how they couldn't go out shopping without being stopped by someone telling Brian how he'd changed their lives.

With all this creativity, of course he'd been an amazing dad too: his three adult children couldn't speak highly enough of him.

When it came to the day of the funeral, it was standing room only.

The service contained tribute after tribute; some wonderful music and the eulogy I'd written, which closed with his wife's choice – a sonnet from Twelfth Night.

I performed it to the backdrop of a hushed, respectful silence: all the while, memories of Brian's early encouragement, ringing in my ears:

Come away, come away, death,
And in sad cypress let me be laid;
Fly away, fly away, breath:
I am slain by a fair cruel maid.
My shroud of white, stuck all with yew,
Oh, prepare it!
My part of death no one so true
Did share it.

There's no way I could have delivered that in public without Brian's input. He'd given me an understanding and love for language which, I believe, changed the course of my life. And in turn, my life's story.

How ironic, that I then got to use this gift to tell his story in return.

And alongside the telling, albeit posthumously, I finally got to say my long-overdue 'thank you' to the amazing Mr May.

A CELEBRANT SHARES

A Hampshire celebrant writes:

* * *

'Don't we see life in our job?

'My last service was for 'a bit of a lad', who was driven in the hearse by an ex-policeman called Griff.

'A fitting end really, seeing as the 'passenger' had been in the back of Griff's police car on such a regular basis when he was alive!'

CHAPTER 6: BURN BABY BURN

On a family visit, I'll always ask if they want the curtains to remain open, or to close around the coffin upon committal: (the formal bit of the service where a body is committed for cremation).

I've lost count of the times people have answered they'd like it closed, 'Because we don't want to see it rolling into the flames.'

When challenged, they swear they, (or a friend), have been to a service and seen the coffin roll away, the fire clearly visible; sometimes even licking up the other side of the door!

I always feel a bit mean shooting them down, but really? Can you imagine a room full of mourners on one side of a door – and naked flames on the other?

What actually happens is the mourners leave the chapel, and then the coffin is pushed off the catafalque, through the hatch, and received on the other side. There, it will wait on a trolley, to be taken off to a separate room that houses the cremators.

Then comes the next frequent urban myth: that everyone is 'done' together. And that coffins are saved and burnt in bulk at the end of the day. Or God forbid, at the end of the week! Again, that's not so.

There is, however, a tight schedule, (which is why crems are so strict about sticking to timeslots). And when a coffin is in the cremator, there's a card on the outside of the machine to say who is in there.

At the end of the process, the remains are cremulated down into ashes, and put into an urn, for their final destination.

This could be an unwitnessed scattering by the crem staff; or a scattering in the grounds, witnessed by family. Or perhaps the family may want to take the ashes off elsewhere, to keep or scatter as they wish. That's the standard choices anyway.

Alternatively, you could roll them into a joint and smoke them, like rappers 'The Outlawz' claim to have done, with their founder Tupac Shakur's remains.

Some families choose to keep a piece of grandma and turn her into 'cremation jewellery'; and others, if you want to go out with a real bang, might choose a company called 'Ascension', who offer to release your ashes up to 100,000 feet on the edge of space.

I particularly loved the story of Mark Gruenwald, the Marvel Comics editor who was so devoted to his job that he requested his ashes were mixed into the printing ink for one of Marvel's titles.

The company obliged his request, and in 1997 reprinted a 1985 collection of 'Squadron Supreme', with Mark, in his widow's words, 'Blended into the very fibre of the book.'

But whatever way they're achieved, obtaining the ashes requires teamwork.

It starts with the undertakers, who have to remove the pacemakers, as they're rather prone to exploding at 850 degrees centigrade. And once certified by a doctor this has been done, they're good to go.

Replacement hips get special treatment too. At my local crem, they're gathered up at the end of a cremation and recycled every six months, with the proceeds going to charity.

Everything behind the scenes is tightly regulated; and it's all accessible – anybody can phone and book a visit, whether that's out of sheer curiosity, or just to put their mind at rest.

Who knows? By the time you get around to a visit, you may see the latest development: resomated water cremations.

Also known as Aqua Cremation/Green Cremation or Bio Cremation, in simple terms, it's high-pressure jets of heated alkaline water, mixed with potash lye, that 'strip' the corpse down, leaving the body's fine bones. Again, these can be ground down and returned as ash to relatives.

Initially, the idea was used in the disposal of infected animal corpses and its pioneers admit it's still a cautious market, (although a local borough, Sandwell are just about to introduce it). But it was the same for the pioneers of cremation in the 19th century.

Developed by an Italian, Professor Brunetti, the idea spread across Europe and North America. In 1879, the UK's first crem was built in Woking. Faced with its mysteries and perceived horrors, the residents protested, which resulted in a temporary ban from the Home Secretary until further legislation was drawn up.

However, in a move you couldn't have invented, the cause was furthered thanks to William Price – a druid and Welsh eccentric – who attempted to cremate his infant son's dead body on a hilltop in Llantrisant.

Although Price was arrested, he successfully argued at his trial the absence of laws stating cremation was illegal; and so, on his acquittal, Woking crematorium began operations without waiting for regulation. Several more crematoria were built in the UK before the Cremation Act was passed in 1902.

As with any new practice, it took decades to be completely accepted, but by the late 1960s, cremations outnumbered burials, and today the figures stand at three to one. But still the myths persist.

So like I said, make an appointment, get yourself down to the local crem and de-mystify the process; it's actually a fascinating experience.

I can't guarantee you'll see my friend Joe reading his Mary Berry cook books in-between cremations, but you'll be guaranteed a warm welcome. No pun intended …

A CELEBRANT SHARES

An 'Ex' confesses all:

* * *

'I've been working with a delightful lady called Louise in order to pull together the service for her neighbour Betty's husband.

'Louise and Betty have known each other for years and are like family. The meeting was very warm, and I spent a lot of time with them both, hearing all about Betty's husband. As a result, I was very confident we'd got all the details in place.

'However, the one detail I didn't have was who Louise is married to. Normally it wouldn't matter, but it really threw me when everyone took up their places on the front row. Sat next to Louise was her husband Aidan, with whom I'd had a passionate relationship for three years, back in my twenties when we were both quite wild.

'Aidan hadn't aged well, but I was really distracted by the memories of how he had looked, and what we used to get up to! I could see him looking me up and down as I read; it was so difficult to focus.

'I'm guessing he didn't say a word to Louise afterwards!'

CHAPTER 7: A GOOD DEATH

Western euphemisms for death:

Pass away
Curtains
A race well-run
Fallen off the perch
Kick the bucket
Gone to a better place
Root inspector
At peace
With the angels
Belly up
Gone to meet their maker
Put on the wooden overcoat
Bumped off
Gone to sleep
Slipped away
Pushing up daisies
Croaked
Departed
Promoted to glory
Pop one's clogs
Taking a dirt nap
Departed

Over the big ridge
Snuffed it
Food for worms
Pegged it
Shuffled off this mortal coil
Born sleeping

Anyone get the idea we're not comfortable talking about death in our western culture?

Whilst we've moved on from the days where illnesses like cancer were referred to in hushed tones as a 'wasting disease', we have a long way to go before people are comfortable with the reality of death.

I'm not suggesting we spend every second of our day obsessed with it, or that we employ the Stoicism school of philosophy founded by Zeno, who suggested that 'we hug our children at night and then tell them tomorrow they might die'; but a mid-way perhaps?

It starts with acceptance; and that's done by incorporating death into our lives as a natural (and inevitable occurrence). One that we talk to children about; that we plan for as we age, and that we acknowledge as we care for our elderly. This would make it easier, and kinder, on everyone in the long run.

But like I say; we've a long way to go. Apart from the fact so many people can't even say the word death, there's a whole culture built up around almost denying it's ever going to happen.

Headlines scream, 'Fifty is the new thirty!' suggesting there are years to go yet. Or 'New Anti-Ageing Pill Promises Longer Life'.

Or perhaps it's more acceptable to go halfway, and acknowledge that death comes to us all, but then buy into the prospect of re-incarnation?

Alternatively, how about being cryogenically frozen? The good news is you can choose whole body, or just your head: and it's only around $90,000! Incredibly, people are actually buying in to this.

As someone who worked in marketing and advertising in the past,

I can't think of a persuasive argument that would sell it to me. 'Don't worry – we'll just wake you up when we've worked out the science bit', perhaps?

Whilst some people think all this talk about dying is morbid, and that we should be focusing on getting on with living, that's all very well. Yes, I agree we should be doing just that, but, whilst we're seizing opportunities left, right and centre: living life to the full: extracting every bit of fun, it should be done with the acceptance that it will one day come to an end.

And when it does – whether that's with a lingering pointless cruelty; with good notice and time to prepare; or with a finality and speed that leaves us breathless; having dealt with our 'stuff' in advance, the landscape would be changed and we'd all be better informed and able to cope.

The dying would have kinder, more supported deaths; and they'd die more often at home; (approximately 50% of people die in hospital, as opposed to the approximate 70% who'd like it to be at home).

Family would be more aware of their wishes, the care they want (or don't want), and there would be the minimum of intrusive or unwanted intervention.

And when death has occurred – because of this clarity and open attitude, families would then benefit in terms of their choices afterwards. Happily, we're moving in the right direction.

Since the mid-1990s, things have steadily been improving, especially with the formation of wonderful charities like 'Dying Matters' (now merged with Hospice UK); a collective of over 32,000 members across England and Wales, formed with the aim of getting people to have these important conversations about death and end of life care.

When ex-footballer Rio Ferdinand's wife died after a short battle with breast cancer in 2015, she was only thirty-four years old. The youngest of their three children was just four.

Rio was understandably devastated, and sought out support via Child Bereavement UK, finding the company of others in a similar situation. And when he was strong enough, he went on to make a documentary for BBC1 entitled 'Being Mum and Dad'.

As part of the documentary he spoke very openly about grief, and his need for support for the children. He talked about how other people deal with it too: the embarrassment around death that causes friends and neighbours to cross the road, because they don't know what to say.

There's a vast army of visionaries, from palliative care workers through to counsellors, hospices, hospitals, community centres and funeral directors that are working to change attitudes just like this.

Two small, but powerful cogs in this army of change are Fran and Carrie, proprietors of the business 'A Natural Undertaking', based in King's Heath, Birmingham.

Not only have they now won 'Modern Funeral Director Of The Year' twice; in 2017, they won an award for 'Best Death-Related Public Engagement Event' with their Brum YODO project. (Brum is the local slang word for Birmingham), so the entire name stands for 'Birmingham You Only Die Once' (www.brumyodo.org.uk)

Through this initiative, via creative and cultural events, festivals, debates, workshops and social media, BrumYODO has been opening up discussions and ending the taboos.

And then, in their normal capacity as undertakers, they also arrange and facilitate the most beautiful services, encouraging family participation before and during, wherever possible.

A great example of this would be a family gathering together over a coffee or a tipple, to decorate a coffin prior to the service. By pasting on family photos, or writing their final messages, it allows them to work together, to reminisce and lay issues to rest. It's not uncommon to see more laughter than tears on these occasions.

Ultimately, it's all about finding ways to bring us closer to how it used to be, when death was talked about, part of the cycle of life, and a 'community' event.

Fran and Carrie have been a huge part of this revolution, but if you met them without knowing, you'd never guess what they did.

Fran is pretty, very delicate and softly spoken. If she'd lived two hundred years ago, she'd have had men flinging their cloaks down over puddles before her, lest she get her delicate feet wet. And Carrie, with her blond hair and rock chick vibe brings the warmth and humour to the duo. With their white funeral car, they're a million miles away from the traditional men in black.

As undertakers, the two of them don't just concentrate on the funeral, but the entire time from death to memorial, and they specialise in funerals that celebrate life, knowing that the choice and the power to take greater control are important when saying our final farewells.

So as well as the usual offering for those that want them; (mahogany coffin; brass handles; one 'slot' at the crematorium); they encourage people to think differently with regards to preparation, service venues, and funeral content.

Whenever I've done a funeral for these ladies, the feedback is incredible. It's not unusual to get people saying they'd like something similar, or that they didn't know 'these things' were possible.

For example, most people think a funeral has to be conducted in a crematorium or a church. Not so! Funerals are not legal events. Registering a death is a legal requirement, and there are laws about disposal of the body, but the ritual of a funeral is not a legality. So you can choose not to have a funeral at all. Or you could hold it in your local village hall; or in a private venue, or even at home. And choosing an alternative venue brings the benefit of an unrestricted time slot too.

You can select a coffin made of wood, or cardboard or wicker. Or no coffin at all; just a shroud. It all boils down to knowing the options, choosing what you want, and telling people in advance what you'd like.

This was exactly what a man called Peter did; and so he got his summer funeral at home, just as he'd requested.

When everyone arrived, Fran and Carrie had already placed Peter in-situ in a wicker coffin, in front of a semi-circle of chairs. A string quartet was playing, and the vibe was very much like a low-key summer garden party. Even more so when everyone was invited to cut a flower from the garden and lay it on the coffin before they took a seat.

I welcomed everyone, then acting in the role of M.C., introduced people, calling them up to give their readings, or offer their words.

Peter's brother gave a touching tribute, then sang 'A Change Is Gonna Come' on his guitar. Friends recounted stories in an easy manner, and I even threw the floor open for last-minute contributions at the end.

The service contained all the anchoring elements that you'd expect, and yes – we did say The Lord's Prayer – because he'd requested it; but the whole event had a sense of freedom and was just so unique.

To end, rather than close on some pre-recorded music, Peter's adult children, (who just happened to be part of a family choir), formed a circle around the coffin, held hands and sang his favourite lullaby: the one he'd sung to them as children. There wasn't a dry eye in the house.

And then, as the service drew to a close, everyone stood and raised a glass of champagne, as Peter was gently lifted, and taken away by Fran and Carrie for direct cremation. It was everything he, and his widow, had wanted.

And it had happened because they'd talked ...

A CELEBRANT SHARES

Sophie from Kenilworth faces a problem lots of us come up against:

* * *

'Help!

'I went to visit a deceased's husband today to gather information. It was like getting blood from a stone. No friends, holidays or career to talk about. Literally all he could tell me about her was that she liked ironing.

'Any suggestions?'

CHAPTER 8: DOING IT RIGHT

One vital requirement for celebrants is the ability to mix with people of all kinds.

I live in a fairly affluent district, but as my experience extended; word spread and enquiries came in from all parts of The Midlands. These covered every area, from wealthy to solid working class, to downright deprived. But regardless of who the clients are, they are all bereaved. They're all paying for a service, and every one of them deserves respect and a service conducted with empathy and compassion.

Having said that, sometimes the physical circumstances can distract somewhat from 'digging deep' and giving it one's all!

Like the time I had to attend a family in a downtrodden part of Tamworth, once a Staffordshire market town that's now become an urban sprawl of inter-connected areas, ring roads and estates.

Tony and Jim's place was a ground-floor flat with more than a hint of Brutalism about it, softened only by the sky-high patch of weeds galloping up the front lawn. I could smell the house before I reached the front door.

I was just about to knock, when the door sprang open. I was greeted simultaneously by Tony (minus his teeth), and the smell of chip fat and tobacco.

"Come on in bab," Tony beckoned. "I've 'ad a bit of a tidy round 'cos I knew you was comin'!"

We walked along the dark corridor to the living room, where I spotted his enormous brother Jim, crammed into a corner, spilling over every inch of his spindly wooden chair.

As I greeted Jim, I trod carefully around a large, heavily-stained mattress in the middle of the floor, to reach the empty chair in another corner.

"Alright bab," said Jim. (It's a local expression. In Scotland it's 'hen'; in Derby it's 'duck'; in Cannock Staffordshire you'd be called 'cocker', and in parts of the Midlands, it's 'bab').

"Don't' mind the mattress," he continued. "It's where we had mom to the end. The council want eighty quid to shift it ..."

He shrugged, despairingly.

As I prepared my notes, ready to start chatting, it was difficult to focus. I was already woozy – no doubt due to the cigarette tar that was literally dripping down the walls. The seat was also sticky, and the room was so cloyingly hot it left me almost gasping for breath.

Seeing I was struggling, Tony offered me some tea, but it was a no-brainer to turn it down. The kitchen area was straight off the lounge and I could see crockery piled up, tea towels on the floor, a bucket full of dirty water and a mop in the sink. It looked like an adventure playground for cockroaches.

I reprimanded myself for being judgmental, as in due course, Tony and Jim turn out to be lovely men. Very open and easy to chat to, although the lack of Tony's teeth did make him a little hard to understand.

We checked the funeral details: (time and venue – very important. Sometimes there are discrepancies and I have nightmares about turning up on the wrong day). And then we started to chat about Annie.

It seemed a fairly pedestrian story at first, but I've learnt from experience to listen intently – you never know when people are going to drop in a bit of a hidden gem.

So I heard the family story, of growing up in a working-class home in the 1930s; with two million unemployed and a thousand people a week dying from influenza. Not that pedestrian at all. But despite the poverty, the brothers remembered lots of love. That always heartens me. If there's not much else to say, then I can at least focus on that as a main theme to the service.

From meeting so many families, I've deduced there's no better foundation than to be valued and loved as a child. You can throw all the money and 'stuff' in the world at a kid, but in the end, as with everyone, we all remember how much time we've been given, and how we've been treated.

So I heard about the games they'd play in the garden: the hide and seek when Annie painstakingly put together trails leading to the hidden 'treasures' for the kids.

And how the family would gather around the piano at the weekends, as they couldn't afford a radio.

And of how she sold her hair to buy Tony his first set of brushes and paints ...

I stopped at this point; knocked sideways at his off-the-cuff statement. There was the gem! It was an old family story: they were used to it, but it was my first hearing. To me, this was a massive gesture of selflessness and love, and deserved further drilling down.

"Yes," he said casually. "Mom was about twenty nine. She had a mane of long thick black hair, and she got a couple of shillings for it. It was enough to buy some paints and brushes for me, and a couple of extra loaves for the week."

"I got bugger all," said Jim.

Alarm bells rang. Just a little, but we were talking over seventy years ago and plainly, there was a memory here that wasn't so good for Jim.

It's not my job to act as a psychotherapist, ('and how did this favouritism affect the rest of your life?'); and I didn't want to witness an argument. What I actually wanted to do was to go back to the enormity of a woman in her late twenties selling her hair in an era of depression, so she could encourage her son's latent talent, and feed the family.

"Ah," I said. "That would have been when everyone was having their hair cut shorter. She took it one step further then didn't she? What a brave move."

I looked up to see Tony with tears in his eyes. Jim had his hand on Tony's. They were sitting immobile, staring at the mattress.

"Doesn't matter," sniffed Jim. "Tony got the paints. But he did the caring for mom in the end. What goes around comes around, eh?"

Tony leapt up at this point and offered to show me his 'art'. I wasn't expecting much as there were no pictures on the wall, (unless you squinted and saw the tobacco stains as some kind of modern offering perhaps). He dashed off to the bedroom and came back with a few canvasses, encased in bubble wrap.

With a deftness and care that surprised me, his long tobac-co-stained fingers delicately peeled back the tape as he removed the wrap. And again, I was staggered. He painted trains. Not my thing, but to my amateur eye, it looked the finest of art.

Tony warmed up then. He told me he was a member of the Guild of Railway Artists. People applied from all over the world, and the standards were exceptional.

He then proudly held aloft his favourite; of a steam train passing through the dramatic sweep of Snowdonia. It actually snatched away the little breath I had left.

"Wow. What a talent. Do you sell them Tony?"

"Here and there," he said. "Some from the Guild. And some to friends. People won't pay what they're worth, but we've just about got enough together now for the funeral. And the next one will pay for the council to take this bleedin' mattress away."

"And we've got our pensions," said Jim, putting his hand back on his brother's. "We'll get there Tone …"

I had to look down at this point. They had bugger all but each other. Never married, no children. They'd lost their mum, and they couldn't even afford for her stained death-mattress to be removed.

I left the meeting, determined that once my head had cleared, I'd put together a damn-good service for them. I just wished they'd not been talked into spending so much on Annie's send-off.

She didn't need a mahogany coffin with brass handles. And she didn't need a horse-drawn carriage. But that's the thing with some working-class traditional families who often have so little. They feel it's the last thing they can do, that it's somehow more 'respectful' to do it, at least in their eyes, 'properly'. Even though, sadly, in the case of Annie, there would be hardly anybody to witness it.

But I was determined to do my bit, and make the focus of the service the family's love for each other. And although they already knew they were cared for, if I could re-iterate it one last time when it mattered, that's what Tony and Jim would take away from the day, and remember forever.

A CELEBRANT SHARES

This one's from an organist colleague at my local crem. He says:

* * *

'Many years ago, when the organ was at the front of the crematorium, it was sited fairly close to the lectern, which made communication between the speaker and myself, fairly easy.

'I was working with a vicar known affectionately as 'Mad Rich': he was quite impulsive and prone to spontaneous outbursts. You honestly never knew what he was going to do next.

'Anyway, on this occasion, as the speaker was doing a tribute, Rich leaned over and in a whisper, asked me if I knew the 'Woody Wood-pecker' theme. I said I did, so he asked me to play it when the speaker had finished.

'I thought it was a bit odd, but he was in charge, so I did as I was asked. The speaker finished, I played 'Woody Woodpecker' (whilst sliding down behind the organ with embarrassment), and then Mad Rich took up his place in front of the microphone again.

'He didn't acknowledge me, or the music, but just continued talking, as if nothing had happened. Woody Woodpecker had no relevance to what he was talking about, and I never got to discover why he asked for it. I must have looked like a complete nutter. What on earth must the congregation have thought?'

CHAPTER 9: DIG IT YOURSELF

Writing the story about Tony and Jim got me thinking about funeral costs.

In March 2019 an average funeral would set you back around £4000. That's a conservative estimate, as it's really hard to find concrete stats, but throw in the addition of extras like flowers, and catering, and really, how many of us could just 'find' that sort of money out of the blue?

But it doesn't have to be like that, if people understand they have choices. And if you're of the mindset to take on much of the 'work', it can cost only hundreds.

That's not something I can ever talk about to clients of course, as by the time I'm in their sitting room, they've booked a funeral director. And I'm the sub-contractor that's working for them. I also understand that many people *do* want to hand over every aspect of the process, and are prepared to pay, so I don't think anyone I work for is likely to go out of business any time soon.

But the reason for including this information is purely to redress the balance, as the authorities are not keen for people to know their options – and at a time of huge distress, that's just wrong.

Half a century ago, it was common-place for the dead to be laid out at home; and for people to visit and pay their respects. If needed at all, a funeral director would only be involved at the final stage; transportation of the body to its final resting place.

A midway for modern times perhaps is a Direct-It-Yourself (DIY) or a Dig-It-Yourself, funeral. A textbook example of this is the sendoff a young man called Mat Hodge arranged for his dad Bill.

With the help of the amazing Natural Death Centre (www.naturaldeath.org.uk), Mat took advice and pulled together a goodbye that not only saved the family thousands, but gave them all huge peace of mind in the process.

Armed with Bill's measurements, Mat ordered a coffin directly from a supplier, and then collected Bill direct from the mortuary. The staff here very helpfully put Bill into the coffin, and then, lid safely screwed on, delivered him to Mat's care at the door. Bill was then transported in the family Vauxhall to a natural burial ground.

It was a process Mat described as, "Daunting, but ultimately exhilarating. Knowing things have been exactly right for you, is an amazing experience. We were so happy with it all."

Wendii Miller was another ordinary person who took on officialdom. Enraged at the 'obstructive' codswallop she was being fed, (especially when she registered the death, and was handed the green form with the words, 'You give this to the funeral director'), ultimately, she collected her mother's body from the mortuary in a camper van herself. She then spent the next three days driving mum around, literally working through her grief.

Wendii said, "I drove Ma to her friends so they could say goodbye. And I took her down to her favourite beach. I very much doubt, being dead, that she was bothered one way or another, but it did ME a helluva lot of good."

Wendy then completed the ritual, digging her mother's grave herself, at her own speed, fortified by tea and chocolate cake supplied by the owner of the burial ground.

Wendii's story was followed by Channel 5, who included it in a TV programme called 'Bizarre Behaviour', which was hugely unhelpful to the cause.

The same with 'Dispatches'; but Wendii remains passionate about the freedom of choice. You can find more on You Tube, (Wendii Miller: A Very Natural DIY (Dig It Yourself) Burial; or Google: The Huffington Post DIY burial/Wendii.

So that's just two stories of how personal involvement can save costs, and soothe the grief. But it all starts with open, frank discussions that allow people to know this stuff well in advance.

In the words of Anna Holmes, who chronicled her sister's care and death in the blog 'Viv' (on the Dying Matters website); 'What are we protected from, when death and dying are professionalised?

How are we diminished by 'parking' death and dying away from our collective selves?'

It's worth more than a thought.

A CELEBRANT SHARES

This celebrant anticipates a good laugh:

* * *

'I have an interesting funeral next Friday for an apparently lovely man with a great sense of humour, who particularly wanted this to happen:

  'The curtains will close as usual, but then a couple of minutes after, the curtains are to re-open, and this time there will be a notice at the end of the coffin saying 'return to sender'.

  Colleague reply:

  'Love it! I had one like that recently: a black coffin, with 'Shit Happens!' engraved on the end!'

CHAPTER 10: LOCAL HEROES

Most of us live pretty ordinary lives. We're not all born to run countries, lead throngs, found institutes and charities and change lives for the better or worse to such a degree that people will know our name for hundreds of years to come.

However, I'd argue that for most ordinary people, their lives may be lived on a less public scale, but they will still experience the kind of ups and downs and extraordinary elements that we see on television every day of the week.

In fact, the more funerals I do, the more staggering stories of bravery, evil, hardship, generosity and love, I see. Lives full of drama that you couldn't make up. It's the stuff of best-sellers!

The colder months are always particularly busy, and sadly, they bring with them a crop of funerals of people in their eighties and nineties. It's a generation the likes of which, I don't think we'll see again.

This was the generation of people who put up and shut up; who got on with life uncomplainingly; because they'd lived through war, rationing, evacuation, the instability of work markets, and so much more. Real hardship. They didn't have the choices the baby boomers and younger people do today.

Many of them have seen loss, illness, poverty and cruelty we can't imagine, so when I have one of these people as a subject, I see it as my absolute duty to give them the send-off they deserve. We should celebrate our elderly, and most-importantly, learn from them, even if it's just humility or gratitude.

For example, the Prussian lady who stowed away on a boat aged fourteen, to find her family in wartime Germany. She walked for three weeks; eating raw turnips from the fields, and wearing the same shoes, because she knew if she took them off – she'd never get them back on again.

I heard of the two sisters who were evacuees in the war. They didn't like the family or the area they'd been sent to; so they decided to walk the hundred miles back to London, by following the train tracks.

And then there's the people who did military service, like the elderly gent who served on the Arctic Convoy when he was young. This was a convoy of ships that sailed first from Iceland, (and subsequently Scotland), around occupied Norway, to deliver vital supplies to the Soviet Union. Perilous journeys Churchill referred to as 'suicide missions', with sub-zero temperatures, and the risk of enemy attack from air and sea.

The Soviets never forgot the efforts of those aboard. In fact, there was a concerted campaign to track down survivors in the 2000s, which resulted in a man called Samuel Greaves getting a surprise visit one day.

So here's the scene: Sam was just pottering around his home on a residential estate in Birmingham. There's a knock on the door, and he opens it to find two Russians, in full military uniform on his doorstep.

(I can't imagine what they must have looked like as they walked through the estate)! Anyway – they present Samuel with a medal for his services to their country.

Samuel's son Mike called him on the phone later that evening. Mike was checking up to see if Samuel had received the planned visit from The British Legion, who were coming to assess his eligibility for a grant to adapt his bathroom. Apparently the conversation went something like this:

Mike: "Dad. Did the British Legion call round today?"

Samuel: "No. But the Russians did."

When Samuel explained the story, Mike said, "Well, I hope you asked them in for a cup of tea."

To which Samuel replied, "Yes, but it was just a quick one. I asked them to go after that, as I was right in the middle of my crossword!"

Mike and I laughed at that when he told it to me; a perfect example of a no-nonsense generation.

A couple of particularly moving services were for the two Commandos I've had the pleasure of talking about. These were the elite fighters, recruited by Churchill. Drawn from the ranks of the British Army, they were described as 'specially trained troops of the 'hunter class' who would develop a reign of terror down the enemy coast'.

Trained at Achnacarry in Scotland, they endured cross-country runs with loaded packs; exercises with live ammunition; speed and endurance marches; river crossings; mountain climbing and unarmed combat. It was a relentless regime, but one that prepared them for the horrors ahead.

In both cases, neither Commando had spoken much to their families about what they'd gone through. That's very typical of most old soldiers, but one of the men had kept a diary for a short while. His family showed it to me, and I found it very touching when I read the page where he spoke of the agony, saying, 'At times it was unbearable. And it was then I called out for my mother.'

The second Commando, an astounding man called Les Whipps, took part in a documentary on their work. He met the journalist Dan Snow. At Les' funeral, Dan sent a personal tribute saying he was a 'legend' and would never be forgotten.

There are stories of absolute selflessness in other ways too – often from feisty old birds like Enid. During the Great Freeze of 1947, while the rest of the country were battening down the hatches, she motor biked to Wales to help the farmers dig out their trapped sheep.

And Elsie, who made it to 102 years old. Her life was a cross between 'Upstairs & Downstairs' and 'A Woman of Substance'. She'd been 'in service' in some of the great houses of the time; she'd lost her mum and two step-mothers to war and illness; raised her siblings, and then her own children. She was still sunbathing topless at seventy, and dancing on tables at family parties into her nineties. What a girl!

And of course, there's the scallywags: like the local family with Peaky Blinders in their history. Legend has it that grandad, (who was a bare-knuckle fighter), wouldn't do a job for the gang, and ended up with an axe in his skull. Unfazed, he then walked to the local hospital for its removal, and lived the rest of his life with an early prototype metal plate in his head. Incidentally, this is also the family claiming to be involved in the theft of the FA Cup the year Aston Villa won. According to them, it was taken and melted down into half-crowns!

Or how about the local councillor in Birmingham who wasn't just a politician, but also a jazz musician, card shark and a gambler?

And finally: all the wonderful women who may appear to have done little in terms of danger or excitement, but who have literally given their entire lives to raising happy, stable families; turning out good human beings who are individuals of worth and value to society.

There are too few people around prepared to do this kind of 'work' today: to do it properly and whole-heartedly. And whether that seems exciting work or not, it's of huge value to wider society. And surely that deserves celebrating just as much as any more outwardly heroic story? The writer Leo Buscaglia summed this up in his eloquent words when he said:

'The majority of us lead quiet, unheralded lives as we pass through this world. There will most likely be no ticker-tape parades for us, no monuments created in our honor.

'But that does not lessen our possible impact, for there are scores of people waiting for someone just like us to come along; people who will appreciate our compassion, our unique talents. Someone who will live a happier life merely because we took the time to share what we had to give.

'Too often we underestimate the power of a touch, a smile, a kind word a listening ear, an honest compliment, or the smallest act of caring, all of which have a potential to turn a life around. It's over-whelming to consider the continuous opportunities there are to make our love felt.'

For adult children of families that have been particularly close, these words are often applicable. But sadly, I also find these families are the ones that seem to handle death the worst. The bonds are so tight it's almost as if the umbilical cord was never cut.

They are also the ones who seem to be least accepting of their parents' deaths. Several times now, I've sat with sons and daughters who are questioning the hospital's treatment of their parents. I hear phrases like, 'Yes, I know she was ninety five, but we've been robbed of those extra years if only they'd done xyz.'

Sometimes, it's hard for people to accept we're human and finite, and the end was coming anyway, (which leads me back to the argu-ment for more openness in all areas surrounding death and mortality).

When I'm talking about people who are so loved, I tend to focus on the themes of sacrifice, tolerance, patience and love. I try to get the families to alter their perspective, from the fact they've lost someone, to being grateful that they've had them in their lives at all. Happily, that's often what's needed to kick-start the healing process, in their own time.

I sat with someone recently who commiserated with me at doing 'such a boring job', but after looking back at the list above, I think it's anything but.

I get to travel, meet all types of people, look inside their homes and lives, and hear all sorts of wonderful stories. Plus, I know what I do is, in some small way, really making a difference.

Who wouldn't want all that on their job description?

A CELEBRANT SHARES

A London Celebrant loses the plot:

* * *

'Just sharing ...

'Today I conducted the service for a lady of ninety-six. She was to be buried with her husband, who passed away eighteen years ago. Everything went smoothly in the chapel, she was transferred back into the hearse and we all took the walk through the cemetery, pulling up a few metres away from the plot: at which point her daughter said, "That's not my Dad's grave!"

'Long story short; I'm returning to the cemetery tomorrow to complete the service when they've located the right place!'

CHAPTER 11: SPIN

No two days are the same, and I love hearing about peoples' fascinating life stories. Sadly though, they're not always true!

Every now and then, a relative decides their loved ones haven't had an interesting enough life; and so posthumously, they decide to get creative – sometimes more than a little.

If a family decides to fabricate someone's history, that's when it can get complicated; but in the celebrant's defence, we can only work with what we've been given.

One of my colleagues, Roy, was halfway through a service, when a man stood up and said, "I'm going outside for a fag. I don't know who you're talking about, but I certainly don't recognise my brother!"

Roy had been expounding about this man's distinguished career in the RAF. He'd spent a couple of hours with the man's widow, hearing all about him. Apparently, she'd been very helpful: full of vivid recollections about his missions, how influential he'd been in the service and how respected he was.

Roy did say later, that maybe the lack of paperwork, (colleague letters, reports etc), should have been a clue; but the wife had been so very helpful, (and convincing), that he'd never thought to question it.

In actual fact, the deceased had been a school janitor! Not to denigrate the role, but it is vastly different, and more importantly, wrong!

We pondered at how someone could simply decide to change a person's life story, and then present it up as fact. Incomprehensible;

especially when all the lies would then be presented for public consumption.

Equally, it was plain as we chatted, that none of the other family members had been invited to attend the meeting with Roy to give their pennyworth. Nope! This funeral was a one-perspective occasion, organised by his wife, and she wanted to hear what she wanted to hear.

Psychologist Robert Feldman claims we all routinely lie. And as well as lying to friends, family and strangers, we definitely lie to ourselves too. It's all about making social interactions go smoothly; but some of us know when to stop, sooner than others.

It's a hugely difficult situation when this happens in such a public way and if it occurs early in your career as a celebrant, it can knock your confidence massively. Who wants to be standing up in front of a group of people, and be brought to task about what they're saying?

A more watered-down version of this is how truths are 'massaged', or sanitised for public consumption. I've slightly more sympathy with this angle – after all, nobody wants their dirty linen aired in public.

Most people in the congregation, if they knew the person well, would know the person's story anyway, but it is interesting how facts can be twisted, bent, adjusted and changed.

A fabulous example was when I met a family who were gathering to remember their dad. Now adults, they recalled how, when they were growing up, the family was split by the parents' simultaneous affairs with a couple of their friends, (those 'irresistible attractions' I mentioned earlier).

The fallout was immense: two of the kids went with one parent, and the other child was separated from his siblings and went to the other home. One half of the family stayed local, and the other child went up North, to a new school, a new set of friends and with a new step-dad to deal with.

It was obvious as he recounted the story, this had had an enormous impact on him. Ultimately, his brothers had been the lucky ones:

they'd had the better life; better home; better school and a happier upbringing, once the dust had finally settled.

And how was all this presented? The answer: in one simple sentence. Referring to the break up and the splitting of the family, it ultimately read like this:

'Eventually, both couples swapped partners, not only on the dance floor but in daily life: bringing new opportunities for all the boys along with it.'

There are lots of other 'shorthand' ways of dealing with all kinds of issues too.

For example: if someone's been in prison, obviously the family will know, but they won't want to major on the fact. I've covered this by saying something like, 'As we all know, Johnny did lose his way for a few years, but ultimately, with the support of his family, he found work/changed his path/made some better decisions.'

Alcoholism is another difficult subject. Someone may have spent a lifetime on the bottle, with all the horrendous fallout that goes with it. But again, mention of alcoholic or alcohol, or even disease, is often verboten. 'Illness' is usually okay though, so I cover it with the words, 'We're all human and fallible. So forgive Donna for her worst as she battled with her illness; and remember her at her best.'

I deal with cold parents with the phrase, 'She was probably more of a practical than emotional mother'. And then for people of a certain age who've led good, but uneventful lives, I talk about them being 'the backbone of British society' (families like that); or 'devoting themselves to raising the next generation of worth.'

The other extreme version from families is simply to slice out huge chunks of peoples' lives. I've lost count of the second wives who say, 'I don't want you to cover any of his life before he met me.'

In these instances, I try to tactfully suggest we get around that using phrases like, 'Michael's first marriage in 1979 didn't endure: but he will always be grateful for his two children Emily and Pete.'

Then, to balance out the mention of the forbidden marriage, I'd segue smoothly into something like, 'However, when he met his soul-mate Nancy, it was a completely different story.' And then Nancy would get several paragraphs about their fabulous marriage. And hopefully that would redress any perceived imbalance.

It also never ceases to surprise me how little some people know about their family's history. One of the things people say most is, 'I wish I'd asked more when they were alive'.

I do my best in those circumstances. I research the times some-one would have lived in, which helps to put together a backdrop to their life story. I encourage people to look at life from that person's perspective and circumstances; which often helps explain why they would have made the choices and decisions they made along the way.

I often ask to speak to others to add a different angle to the service – such as work colleagues or old friends. It's very gratifying to unearth a story that the family didn't know, and so another piece of the jigsaw slots into place. And a huge portion of the time, it's absolutely worth the effort; as summed up by the following email:

'Thank you so much. You are very good at what you do. I'm per-sonally grateful to you for asking some very intriguing questions and helping me to realise that, even though my uncle's life seemed sad and solitary to me, he had made his own choices over the years. He was happy in his own way and, as you so rightly pointed out, he hurt nobody.

'You helped me realise that there are many ways to live a happy and fulfilled life. A valuable lesson learned at a sad time.'

A CELEBRANT SHARES

One of my own gems:

* * *

'I was visiting a lady to talk about Clive, her partner of forty one years. They'd lived very small lives and were happy with it, but as always, it makes for slim picking when you're trying to pull together a service.

'However, she did brighten up when I asked if he had a sense of humour. She then laughingly told me about the 'hilarious' story of how he went into work one day, and severed off half a finger!

'This was quickly followed up with the rest of the story: how she got a call from the hospital, dashed over, and arrived just in time to see the surgeon, who informed her the finger could be saved. But Clive had other ideas, saying, "Ah – just get rid of it. It's less trouble."

"And do you know what," she informed me, through tears and sad smiles, "It really brought us together."

Bewildered and curious, I asked, how on earth?

"Well," she'd continued gleefully, "Every Christmas from then on, I used to make him a little Santa hat for the stump! God, we had a laugh over it!"

CHAPTER 12: RULES!

Currently, being a celebrant is an unregulated profession, as is that of a funeral director.

People don't tend to think about that do they? When you hand over your loved one to the men in black, we all just assume things will be done properly and respectfully, to a set of industry standards.

Thankfully, it generally is, but I'm sure, in both the world of funeral directors, and celebrants, there will always be some who do it better than others.

It's very different at the crematorium though, where for celebrants and ministers, it becomes Rules City!

It begins on the walls of the vestry, (the waiting and changing room for clergy and celebrants), which are papered with lists of instructions. And just in case we forget them, they're also stuck onto the podium in the chapel, in large letters on yellow paper.

It's utterly mind-boggling when you're a new celebrant, trying to manage the service, remembering what buttons to press (or not press) for curtains and music; all whilst sticking to the timings, not tripping up over family names, controlling your emotions, and looking calm.

The rules vary depending on the venue, but at my local one we're instructed that:

WE MUST run through the order of service, (the content and the order it's happening in), with the chapel attendant prior to delivery; as sometimes families change things at the last minute.

To this end, we always check music choices and what order they're to be played in. And vital, vital, vital – double check whether the curtains are to stay open or be closed at the end.

The thinking about curtains is that if they close around the coffin, the person is leaving you, and it's literally a goodbye. Some families think this abhorrent, and prefer to leave them open so they can touch the coffin on the way out. But again – they often worry it's them doing the 'leaving' of the person they loved.

I've had hideous moments when this has been changed last-minute and not got the message. I'll never forget closing them as a woman leapt up and screamed, "Nooooooo. Bring him back. Bring him back."

Other rules …

WE MUST allow five minutes for entry into the chapel, and five minutes for exit.

This is always hard to time as people never really know how many mourners are going to turn up. Sometimes all the mourners are inside within two minutes. And sometimes we're still waiting, with the FDs running around trying to find everyone seating, fifteen minutes later. Those services always create rising panic inside, as I mentally run over what bits I can cut out without anyone noticing.

We also **MUST NOT** over-run our allotted time as the funeral directors (and then the families) will be charged for an extra slot.

If it's a thirty-minute service, then providing people enter in time, that's enough for a welcome, a eulogy and a short piece of music in the middle, according to the crem 'rules'.

In reality, it's actually all down to how long the eulogy takes. Some are over in three minutes, and others can take twenty. You can be left with an incredibly short service, or one that's galloping wildly to the thirty minute mark with the family speaker showing no sign of drawing to a halt. This is where the skill of managing the timings and planning beforehand comes in.

I've also learnt never, if at all possible, to allow anyone to get up and read anything if I haven't seen it beforehand. Some people's idea of a speech taking 'just five minutes' is frankly frightening. And so, if I can't persuade them to hand over the goods, then I warn them severely of the consequences if they do over-run. (And yes – I have had to step up and stop someone in their tracks, which is just awful).

But believe me, there's nothing more intimidating than an FD standing at the back of the room, doing 'cut throat' signs because things aren't panning out. It makes my heart sink, because when they do this, you know the prospect of more work is now horribly threatened because they don't rate your timings.

We also **MUST NOT** shake hands with mourners inside the chapel, as this encourages them to linger too long; creating a bottleneck, encroaching on the service that follows immediately after.

Instead, we're instructed to move well along, through the exit door and outside, to the area where the flowers are displayed. (I usually exit halfway through the final piece of music to take a deep breath and steel myself for the hand-shaking to come).

That's always a difficult bit. Some people come out and make a beeline to shake my hand. They tell me the service was wonderful, or moving, or they ask how long I'd known the deceased? (That brings me a little flutter of joy, as I consider it a real compliment to think I spoke sincerely enough for people to assume I was a friend).

Then there are others who deliberately avoid me; their eyes darting to the flowers, or the signs on the walls that warn about the possibility of said flowers being eaten by wild rabbits. Anything but engage me in conversation.

And sometimes they come out with a mission, (sorry, but it's usually devoutly religious people), who are affronted that this particular service didn't contain a hymn or a prayer.

Just for clarification at this point, I have to say again that I do whatever is required by the family. If it's a non-religious service, then it contains no spirituality, God or any mention of the afterlife. (I know one humanist who is so strict they won't even allow the Robbie Williams song 'Angels' to be played!)

However, as an independent civil celebrant, I'm not committed enough either way to feel strongly about it. So if someone wants no religion that's fine. And if they want The Lord's Prayer, or Jerusalem, or whatever; that's fine too.

But it's not my choice, it's for the family to decide. And in most circumstances, the service is put together to reflect the person we're there to remember. If they weren't religious, never went to church, or didn't have any kind of faith, then why pretend they did?

In these circumstances, I usually settle things during my welcome words and explain that the service will reflect the deceased, and the family's wishes. And so it will be full of warm memories, recollections and stories, all designed to bring a smile to the faces of those they loved.

That's usually enough to manage expectations and get people ready for a lovely, warm and personal thirty minutes. But every now and again I get somebody sliding up to me who just can't contain themselves.

At the end of one service, a man shot past me, and practically hissed, "Interesting service. And where was Jesus????!" as if I was the Devil incarnate. I simply told him that on this particular day, God hadn't been invited.

Another lady came up and announced that she was a Christian, and she'd now have to go home and spend some time in dedicated prayer to rectify the 'gross negligence' I'd imposed upon the poor man's soul.

And yet another lady, ('born again' this time – like my mum was), came up and said she'd actually quite enjoyed it, and how personal it was, but "Here's my card anyway. I feel you're missing out by not knowing The Lord. I could be the one to introduce you properly to him."

As someone who watched her own mum get to know Jesus fairly well at a late stage in her life, believe me, I was in no rush.

Mum was one of the worst type of Sunday Christians: judgmental, narrow-minded and intolerant of others' choices. This was the woman who once wrote to the local newspaper, asking them to 'investigate the possibility of lesbian teachers' at the local college!

She followed her religion blindly, interpreting what she wanted as she went along, oscillating wildly between ridiculous faith: (praying about whether to have a new carpet, and then when a furniture van went past the window, taking it as a 'sign'); and proclamations of eternal doom: 'You'll go to hell for being promiscuous!'

She also placed her faith in God when she got cancer; refusing treatment because God would sort it out. And I remember going to her funeral six months later.

Strangely enough, I also remember not being particularly helpful to the officiant doing my mum's service. My brother had a few kinder things to say than I had, but it was still pretty hard work for the poor woman. I remember that scenario every time I sit with a family who are short on information to give me. And in truth, because I've been there myself, I can't get annoyed with them over it.

But yes; I'd say overall, most people do want to come up and shake my hand at the end of a service. Which reminds me of the final rule at the crematorium, this time a self-imposed one.

I **MUST** remember to take along the gel handwash. Shaking hands, especially during winter flu-season, is quite a risky business.

At the end of some of the better-attended services, my hands touch hundreds of others. Along the way, my fingers have been left smeared in anything from biro ink, through to eczema scabs, food remains and traces of other peoples' snot …

A CELEBRANT SHARES

This poor celebrant had no preparation time at all for the service:

* * *

FLYING BY THE SEAT OF THE PANTS

'I was just leaving the crematorium today, when the chapel attendant stopped my car and asked breathlessly if I could do another service!

'The vicar for the next one had totally forgotten, and was at least an hour away. He didn't use the internet so there was nothing he could send over by email. There was a full chapel and some understandably irate and distressed mourners.

'With just over ten minutes' notice, I somehow managed to take the service, pulling on every ounce of professionalism, guts and nervous energy I possessed. There was no way I could have turned them down.

'Afterwards, the family said they were very pleased and the FD, who has never used me before, told me I would be on his list from now on.

'Crikey – no two days are ever the same are they?'

CHAPTER 13: DIGNITY AND DECORUM

When you stand at the front of the chapel, you're really on show. Not only because of the physical proximity to everyone, but also because of the nature of the job.

It's both gratifying and terrifying; people hang off your every word. But it also means there's huge potential for embarrassment, as everything is noticed. Some things we have control over, and others not; but whatever the reason for them happening; every tiny faux pas or incident will be spotted.

One of the most embarrassing events during one of my services wasn't actually down to me, but caused by the arrival of the widow, decked out in her yellowing wedding dress and tiara. She had no family to advise her of just what a bad idea this was: the mourners literally gasped as she got out of the hearse.

I 'managed' this by saying, at the appropriate time in the eulogy, what a close marriage they'd had, 'As evidenced by Stella's choice of clothing today.'

This led nicely into the reflection music, which had been their first dance song. But then Stella leapt up, and performed some sort of Kate Bush-style contemporary dance around her husband's coffin. I stood at the front, frozen with horror, just speechless. But rather weirdly, it was a perfect set up for the following poem, that urged us to 'Rage, rage against the dying of the light'.

An equally embarrassing time, for a completely different reason, was being caught short with irritable bowel syndrome one minute before a service. For anyone who doesn't 'get' this, I'll sum it up by saying, it's the condition that takes no prisoners and offers no choices.

Remember the athlete Paula Radcliffe, squatting to take a dump on live TV in the middle of the 2005 London Marathon? Given any alternative but that, I'm sure she'd have taken it, but when you gotta go, you gotta go.

On one particular day, when I couldn't trust my nether regions, after a rather, let's call it 'unsatisfactory' visit to the loo, I had no choice but to stuff a ton of paper in my knickers, and hope for the best.

Things were uncomfortable from the moment I took up my place in front of the coffin to walk the procession in.

This is always a pivotal moment in a service anyway, as I can't see behind me, and I can't judge how fast to 'lead'.

Different teams of bearers travel at different paces. Some walk with a slow, dignified gait, every footstep matching, like pairs of well-trained carriage horses. Sometimes a team will make it a brisker pace, a bit how men tend to walk past a jewellery shop window when their girlfriend's been dropping hints.

And I swear, there's one team who treat it more like a winter toboggan race, especially if the coffin's being brought in on a trolley on wheels. I've walked in front of these guys before and they've almost taken the skin off the backs of my ankles!

But on this particular day, it was dignified and slow. Which wasn't great for me, as almost immediately, I felt the wad of toilet paper working its way down my trouser leg. I could really have done with a sprint to the lectern, in order to hide the wad, but had no choice. I just clenched my thighs together, and waddled up slowly.

Thankfully I made it with the loo paper in situ. If it had escaped down my trouser leg and landed on the aisle, in front of everybody, it would possibly have been my last-ever service.

The wad stayed at mid-knee level, but it was fully-visible as I left the chapel, looking as if I'd developed elephantiasis leg.

Other awful moments include the day I was 'breaking in' my new dental braces. Unfortunately, the wire was too long at the side and had literally drilled a little hole into my cheek, giving me an ulcer.

Barely able to speak, I opened my mouth to read the eulogy, and watched horrified as a long rope of bloody saliva descended, attaching itself from the corner of my bottom lip, straight on to my folder, like a germ-ridden zip wire.

I was standing just 4' from the mourners, who were all beauticians. These ladies were trained with laser-like precision to notice an erupting blackhead at twenty paces. There was no way they missed that one!

The same with running noses, due to emotion or a cold. Always when your head's down, gravity steps in. The only thing to do is to try and sniff it back during the music for reflection.

For me, this slot is a bit like a lay-by on a motorway when you've a punctured tyre. You know it's coming up, and just hope you can hang on long enough to get there.

Having said that, I know it's not just me. Along the way, my colleagues have shared similar stories. One performed an entire service with a sticky label saying 'Reduced' on her jacket; and others with flies open or bits of loo roll trailing from their shoes. And of course there's always the hazard of food on the teeth to contend with.

Some things are so plain random you simply couldn't anticipate them; like the poor colleague who was at the most solemn of moments, bowing to the coffin, when her stiletto heel snapped off.

And then there's the mistakes waiting to be made as you're speaking. It doesn't matter how professional someone is, every now and again we all make them. Even something as simple as an overhead light shining on the plastic folder containing your words, can alter your perspective and make the words hard to read.

However, sin number one has to be getting the name wrong. You'd think it would be easy enough when it's written down, but not always. For example, when there's a string of words with the same letter, it's easy to trip up. In one family, the sisters were called Jean, Joan, Jane and June. I really had to focus to remember the deceased was Joan.

Another time, I found myself saying that I committed Beryl's 'botty' for cremation.

And how about the family of a lady called Evelyn Male, who asked me not to mix it up with our local paper, 'The Evening Mail'.

But the most excruciating time was when I recited the Lord's Prayer: something I've done hundreds of times before; but not generally with a migraine.

Thanks to some really heavy-duty tablets, I was able to stop the migraine in its tracks, but the side-effects were brain fog and a very, very dry mouth. Not ideal for leading a service, but I trooped on, hoping for the best.

I was doing quite well until I got to the Lord's Prayer, which on this particular day, didn't seem to 'scan' properly to me. About one third of the way through, I felt rising panic, as I realised I hadn't got a clue what came next.

Hence, out of my mouth came a jumbled combination of lines, during which I asked The Lord to, 'Protect us from our evil bread!'

Without exception, every single head in the room shot up at once. I wanted to fall through the floor.

Thankfully though, it became more of an amused talking point on the way out. This was evidenced by the bright spark, who winked and shook my hand as he left. And his parting shot?

'Pitta about the Lord's Prayer love. But you'll be back on a roll in no time.'

Genius!

A CELEBRANT SHARES

So many dreadful moments. These are all mine. Hopefully if I dump them on the page they'll leave my mind and stop haunting me:

* * *

'Getting my roles mixed up. At weddings I say congratulations. And at funerals it's condolences. But congratulating a man on the death of his son was just horrendous …

'Being approached at the end of the wake by the widower (in his seventies), who didn't seem all that grief-stricken. He suggested it might be nice, due to my love of music, if we 'caught a gig together sometime.' This invitation was accompanied by a gentle squeeze on my left nipple: all in full view of the mourners at the golf-club bar.

'Visiting a family for the third time. Wondering how I could make the service different from the previous two, I joked that I felt 'A bit like Liz Taylor on her eighth wedding night. I know what to do, but I'm not sure how to make it interesting.' They didn't laugh.

'Reading a twenty-seven verse Max Boyce poem (at the widow's request), in a Welsh accent. This raised not one single laugh through-out the whole, crappy thing. Although to be fair, my ego did feel slightly less bruised when a lady came out at the end, and in a strong

Welsh accent said, 'Not bad. Not bad at all love. I'd have placed that at Mid-Glamorgan!'

'Conducting a service for a Spanish man called Jesus. He was a writer, so I dubbed him 'Jesus of Narrative'. Nobody laughed at that either.

'The curtains closing on committal, but then grinding to a halt halfway around the coffin. And there they stayed. I just couldn't think of a solitary appropriate thing to say at that moment.

'Bowing to the coffin at the end, walking out in a dignified manner and, as usual, reaching for my coat, which was draped over the fire extinguisher by the exit door. On this one occasion it was tangled through the hose and the spray mechanism and I had to pull so hard that the extinguisher clattered to the floor.

Yes: of course everybody saw'.

CHAPTER 14: THIS IS NOT MY GRIEF

People ask, 'How can you do this? Doesn't it affect you terribly?'

The honest answer is that it could, but I can't afford to let it, because I'd be doing a disservice to my families.

Look at it another way. If you had a sick child in a hospital, would you want the nurse weeping over the bed alongside you, immobile with sadness? Or would you want them to be of the 'chin up, we can get this sorted' persuasion?

That's how I can be of help to families. Being their 'nurse' for the duration; gently guiding, listening to them and ultimately, putting together personalised, meaningful services that help them begin the healing journey. As I say in my leaflets, nobody should leave a service feeling angry, ignored or ill-served.

If I do feel myself getting drawn in on the day, then there are several methods. One is to tell myself I'm acting in a play, and my storyline is to be the strong and masterful celebrant.

Another method, (as preferred by Prince Charles, I believe), is to bite the inside of my cheeks if it's during part of the service when I'm not speaking. I also try not to look directly at the family too often.

Obviously, making eye contact and giving an encouraging smile every now and then is vital – there would be no connection at all if I didn't do that. But when I see a row of faces, crumpled with grief and hollow with shock, there's part of me that could easily be drawn in if I didn't step back quickly.

We spent an entire day during training looking at how to deal with especially harrowing scenarios. When I'd initially signed up for the course, I imagined it would be mainly dealing with run of the mill scenarios such as an eighty five year-old lady dying after a full and satisfying life; because that's how we tend to envisage death from the outside. None of us, unless we're directly involved, really think much about the detail.

But when we sat in the classroom and turned to the next page in the manual, entitled, 'Extraordinary Circumstances', we entered the world of children and baby deaths, suicides and murders. And believe me, you do need to be made of strong stuff to sit in front of a family under those circumstances.

There are never the 'right' words. I just find it's best just to listen and talk to people as normal human beings, rather than offer platitudes and amateur psychology. But the aim at the end of the family meetings is still to produce a service that will offer comfort and help people to move on.

This is particularly difficult in the case of children; a call we all hate to receive. Losing a child is something no parent should have to go through, and it doesn't matter what their age, the grief felt is the same.

I held the hand of an 83 year old lady saying goodbye to her 51 year old daughter who'd suffered dreadfully with diabetes. My heart ached for her as she sat in her wheelchair, in a windswept burial ground, sobbing quietly how she'd always just 'thought she'd get better'.

I remember one case I was particularly touched by, when a 23 year old man, in the prime of his life, was knocked over by a lorry at his place of work.

He'd gone off that morning, leaving behind a trail of clothes: the radio blaring; chocolate wrappers in the kitchen and a note telling them what time he'd be back later.

And then came the call. I can't imagine how it must have been, to go to the site, and see the incident tent erected over his body, but not be allowed to see him. To have to wait until the police and fire services had finished their work before they could. To deal with the grief of his eight year-old sister. And to know he'd left a three year-old daughter fatherless. The repercussions, as with any family, go on and on.

That particular service is one that will stay with me forever. Not only for the sadness of the circumstances, but the sheer strength of his mum Diana: an elegant, beautiful woman in her mid-forties.

I remember the day so clearly. The searing summer heat, and the greenery of the crematorium grounds. The trees were in full bloom, forming a vivid backdrop to a sea of people in black, with grey, pallid faces. I remember the juxtaposition, like a piece of pop art, sepia on green. And the quiet … nobody talking. Not a soul.

The only time I've come across an eerie silence like that was when I visited Belsen in the 1980s. There, no birds flew across the grounds, and people walked like zombies around the visitor centre, displaying a palpable sense of horror. And that day, it felt the same. At twenty three, you think you're invincible. And suddenly, everyone knew they weren't.

It took about fifteen minutes to get everyone into the chapel, and after my introduction, I asked Diana to come up and speak. I think it's always best if we can start a service with personal contributions (if the person feels strong enough to do it): not only because ultimately, they are the people who knew the subject best, but also, because it gets it out of the way for them. They don't have to spend the entire service dreading having to get up. It's over and done, and then they can sit back down and be supported by those around them.

When Diana approached the lectern, she was clutching a sheet of paper so hard, her knuckles were white. She literally stood there, trembling from head to foot, snatching tiny gasps of air, until she could eventually speak.

'I had no idea Martin had so many friends. Thank you all for coming. I've heard him speak about some of you, but now I'll be able to put faces to names.

'Martin was too young. His life was cut short, and with it, ours have been too. We'll go on for the sake of his sister, and his daughter, but we'll never see him marry or have more children, and I can't describe the heartache that brings us.

'We'll never know where his career could have taken him, but really, it's not about jobs and money is it? It's about people; friends and family. 'And you're here today, so thank you. Seeing so many of you gives me comfort that his memory and his stories will go on.

'But don't let it end there. Make some new stories for him too. Take him with you on your lads' holidays and boys' nights out. Take him with you in your hearts on your stag nights and to your weddings. Talk about him at the most important times of your lives. Involve him and laugh and smile at the memories. It will help us to know that his presence is missed.'

I don't mind admitting, on that occasion, after the service, I sat in my car and howled my eyes out. In a corner, parked under a tree where nobody could see me.

And when every last drop of sadness was expelled, I took a deep breath, re-applied my make-up, checked my watch for timings, and made my way across the city to see the next family.

Always ready to drop in when needed, and then leave when the work is done. A bit like Mary Poppins.

A CELEBRANT SHARES

A rookie error:

* * *

'So embarrassed! I was standing outside in the flower garden, to greet the mourners as they came out from my service, when a man came bearing down on me with a £10 note.

'I've never taken a cash tip, as I just feel uncomfortable about it – just wouldn't feel right. So as he got near I smiled and said something like, 'Ah that's lovely, but really it's okay. You don't have to.'

'He looked at me and said, 'But I want to. Really.'

'I put my hands up to stop him and smiling, I said, 'It's a lovely thought, but you really don't have to, honestly.'

'He looked annoyed then and almost growled at me, 'But I WANT TO!' Before I could say anything else, he lunged forwards. I thought he was going to hit me! But in a split second, I realised that wasn't the case. He was merely trying to get his £10 into the donations box that I was standing directly in front of!'

CHAPTER 15: THE DEVIL'S IN THE DETAILꞱ

As well as realising that every client, regardless of their circumstances, deserves a job well done; another learning was never to think you know it, or have seen it all; no matter how long you've been in the business.

Apart from the fact we're dealing with people and by that definition, it's a random business, there's always something new. If you're a good writer, you can write better, more eloquently, more succinctly or descriptively. If you have a tendency to preach, then it can be curbed and turned into storytelling instead, which is so much more palatable.

If you empathise too much, then you have to stop, because depression or sadness will creep in and it can get you down in the end. Or if you're a bit too detached, then learn from that, warm up a little and put yourself in those poor peoples' shoes.

Even things as simple as assuming the route to the crem will be clear on the day is a big mistake. You have to factor in time for an accident, a road closure or roadworks: it's just not worth the stress of sitting in the car wondering if you're going to make it.

One of my particular learning curves was about fact-checking. Each and every time. You'd think as a trained journalist this would be second-nature, but it's easy to get complacent after so many years.

With regards to the service wording, I know some celebrants don't let their families see anything beforehand, but that's not my style. I also think the families deserve to know what's being said in advance. It relieves them of stress on the day, so nobody's sitting there thinking

'Oh God, what's coming next?' as so often, people wish they had, or hadn't said something during our meeting.

For this reason, I think it's best all round to let them see every word and that way, nobody can make any accusations or claim to have been short-changed.

However, even if they do see the wording, there's always deemed, (by the family at least), to be room for a last-minute contribution or addition. This often happens when they're an indecisive bunch, or perhaps someone decides to shoehorn in a personal tribute; or a distant relative suddenly offers up a long-lost memory that's vital to include.

Peter and George were a great example. Two brothers who'd lost their mum; the initial meeting was with them and their wives, one sunny August evening in Staffordshire. And delightful though they were, it would be generous to say they were more than a tad ponderous.

Both excelled in the art of verbosity. Using twenty words where four would do, they delivered every syllable as if they were learning a foreign language … veeeery slooowly in ooooorder to make shuuure it's all understooood prop-er-ly.

That meeting is four hours of my life I'll never get back, but it did result in another learning. So for that reason I have to, as I say in my services, 'be grateful'.

So there we were, settled in their garden in the fading sunlight, me with my writing pad at the ready, and 'the boys' and their wives with glasses of wine in their hands.

They batted ideas for music backwards and forwards, reminiscing about how they used to march up and down the garden as young boys with their swords and home-made shields to Wagner's 'Ride of The Valkyries'. "Perhaps mum should come in to that," said Peter.

"Or Chas and Dave," suggested George, "because she could 'Rabbit'!"

They all fell about laughing, taking several minutes to recover. I sighed inwardly, knowing it was going to be a long night. I think bats were actually circling at dusk when I managed to steer them away from the music discussion (something a family can always do without me), to the information I really did need about their mum.

And eventually I learned what an accomplished woman Celia was. She painted; sewed; cooked; took in all the neighbourhood kids; fed everyone and was an all-round good egg.

They talked enthusiastically for almost two hours, during which I never stopped scribbling.

Cats cropped up many times during the conversation – she owned several, and adopted and fed others. I clearly got the message that Celia loved cats.

It was pitch black when I left them all, in a merry mood, high on the grape and the memories. For my part, I got back home starving, texted my then boyfriend to apologise for not making it over to see him; whilst also apologising to my border terrier Gloria, who was looking decidedly grumpy at the lack of company.

I let her into the garden, and idly watched her pee for a full minute, poor animal. She was plainly desperate to get out, so although I was exhausted, I relented; and for the next half hour we strolled around the block as paragraphs, ideas and phrases about Celia swirled around my head.

I had a couple of difficult patches whilst planning the flow of the service, trying to work out where their ex-sister-in-law would speak, (she wasn't offering up any clues about content, but assured me it would be no more than five minutes). And so, having left an open slot for her, I duly sent off the wording for approval.

Peter sent back a very nice note saying how I'd 'clearly put hours of considered effort into this, and we're very grateful'. He mentioned again about his mother's love of cats, ending with the phrase 'a love she particularly shared with her son George'. He asked me to make sure I covered this love of cats and make it prominent in the service. Then, almost as an aside, he told me I'd be getting a couple more contributions from other family members.

These arrived just the night before the event; at almost 11pm. To say I was pissed off would be an understatement.

One was from the grand-daughter mentioning how they always used to buy Celia a stuffed toy cat when they were little and on holiday. And one from a niece, with a small story about watching television with Celia, and echoing the cat sentiment again.

In all honesty, I could have done with the information sooner. It's far from ideal to be fiddling around with the wording just twelve hours before the service, but I incorporated the new stories, and it all fitted well. My mistake was not to send it for final, final, final approval.

So there we are on the actual day. The coffin comes in with a toy stuffed cat sitting on top of it. I wait for everyone to settle before beginning the service, and I start with the welcome. I talk about Celia's love of cats. I point out the cat on the coffin. I'm doing well I feel.

At the right section, I invite Peter up, and he gives a rather random tribute to his mum (he reads out the sympathy cards), during which the lens of his glasses pops out. Everyone laughs good-naturedly, as he's a bit of a klutz, but a loveable one.

At this stage, I start to suspect he's high-functioning autistic, or at least on some spectrum, (a bit like Al, the man who 'had' King Lear in him). But not to worry: it's all going well until I'm about halfway through the eulogy, when Peter loudly calls me over to the front row.

"Nooooo! That's not it. That's not right! Come over here!"

I look up, startled. The blood feels as if it's draining from my body. Hundreds of people are now gawping at me in shock. I'm actually being heckled in a crematorium!

I totter over on the jelly legs, wondering what on earth was coming next. Everyone's eyes swivel to follow me. I lean over to Peter and in hushed tones ask, "Is everything OK?"

"No," he booms, making no attempt to match the volume of my question. "It's not OK. You haven't mentioned my mother's love of cats – a love she particularly shared with her son George."

"I have. In many ways," I assured him.

I leapt back to the podium, and joked something about 'taking notes from my director.' People laughed politely, but Peter still didn't look happy. Then suddenly, it dawned on me that he needed to hear those exact words. In that exact order. Otherwise, for him, the service wouldn't be complete.

I managed to squeeze them in elsewhere, and although they stuck out like a sore thumb, (I'd not exactly had time to work them into the service smoothly), I saw his shoulders drop back down and relax.

The next issue came when the ex-sister-in-law got up to speak about Celia. Helen was eloquent and captivating, and obviously adored Celia, but she over-ran her allotted timeslot by fifteen minutes!!

Fortunately, by dropping some of my lines at the end, I managed to make it all fit. But this was the service when it really came home to me how important it is to vet and check absolutely everything people want to do.

And thankfully, Peter was ultimately happy with it all. He e-mailed six weeks later, to thank me for my sensitive handling of Helen's errant timings, and for my warm delivery of his beloved mum's service.

And in return, I sent him a thank you card with a cat on.

A CELEBRANT SHARES

A story to prove we all love a bargain, from a Cheltenham Celebrant:

* * *

'I saw a man today about his deceased wife. He seemed really agitated at the meeting. I tried to get him to relax, to tell me some proper stories, but in the end he admitted he 'hadn't got time'.

'Apparently, he was in a rush and needed to get to M&S before closing, as it was the last day he could return his wife's clothes for a refund!'

CHAPTER 16: TAKING OFF

I have to admit, when I entered the profession, I'd no idea it was so competitive.

I left my training feeling as if I could conquer the world; but with the discovery of fifteen-plus organisations churning out celebrants, my early confidence just evaporated.

I'd knocked tentatively on a few FDs doors; been received with brusque indifference, and that was all it took for confidence to be replaced with self-doubt and fear. Fear that I didn't have what it took, or worst of all, that nobody would take me seriously.

It occurred to me how strange it was that after so many battles won, here I was in my early fifties, now doubting myself again.

Wasn't I the woman who'd held audiences in the palm of her hands in the eighties, doing stand-up? And who'd sailed the high seas, interacting with thousands of passengers a week, in the nineties?

What on earth was wrong with me?

"It's just that you were younger then," said my no-nonsense friend Kaz.

"This getting old business is shit. We're all in the same boat. Menopausal, forgetful, sleep-deprived and terrified we're going to be found out."

I had to laugh. She'd hit the nail on the head. Now officially invisible, and seemingly unemployable, I was struggling to make sense of it all.

But ultimately, it was the fear of being trapped in financial penury and jobs I hated, for the rest of my life, that made me power through.

At the time I was self-employed and working for a local ad-agency. I just couldn't continue with the tedium of copywriting and producing blog posts for their small business clients.

For a Tarmac company I'd come up with things like: 'The History of Tarmac'; 'Does Your Home Have Kerb-Appeal?' and 'Ten Fun Facts About Tarmac'.

For a conveyor belt manufacturer I'd written about quality control at their plant in China; and for a hairdresser, a blog entitled 'Hair Extensions. Am I too old to go long?'

But the Eureka moment came halfway through a blog on manicures for dogs, when I found myself screeching, "Bollocks. Just bollocks. No! I've had enough," at the wall. I may also have thrown a cup of tea …

And so, without any real plan, I marched to the wardrobe; grabbed my suit; went to the supermarket and purchased boxes and boxes of shortbread, and began what I now know is called, 'The Biscuit Run.'

Over three days, I knocked on the doors of twenty four funeral parlours. Some FDs and arrangers saw me, and some didn't. Some asked me to make an appointment and return. Everyone took my card, (even though I knew some would go straight in the bin). I kept knocking, talking, handing out biscuits and hoping. And eventually, the phone rang.

It wasn't a quick build by any stretch, and at times I didn't really know if I'd be able to keep afloat, but in due course things took off to the point where I could drop the blogs forever.

I was also really keen to spread the word about celebrants: taking any opportunity available to talk at WI meetings; hospices; local interest groups – you name it. Not just to find work of my own, but to inform people of what we do, to increase awareness for the future market.

Having said that, there's still some way to go. People still ask, when they leave the crem, what I am (even though my name and title is printed inside the order of service).

I went on a family visit a while back and the man (confusing me with a Humanist and a celebrant), said to his family, 'Switch the telly off – the celebratory human's here!'

On other occasions, I've been called a 'celibate' (of course) – easy mistake. But the best phone call has to be when someone rang me up to tell me he and his wife were celebrating twenty-five years of marriage, and in my capacity of 'humanitarian' could I officiate at their 'vowel' renewals?

But whatever we're called, it's just good word is getting out there about the role; and that work finally started coming in.

After my hundredth service, it dawned on me that celebrancy was now my 'proper' job. It took a while to sink in that after all the effort, I could possibly make a living from it.

Then the level cranked up again. Two hundred services became three, then four hundred. Free evenings became a thing of the past, and 10pm finishes were normal.

Weekends disappeared; swallowed up with visits to families who couldn't see me any other time. My home became a meeting place for others, gathering from afar, who had nowhere else to go. It wasn't unusual to be seeing up to nine people in the living room, giving them tea, biscuits and a shoulder to cry on.

I started to cancel evenings with friends. And my vague attempts to try and date went by the wayside. There was always a funeral or a wedding; an interment of ashes or a vow renewal. I was always seeing families; at a venue, or busy writing the next service.

Exhausted, I called Kaz to complain, but she was having none of it.

"This is exactly what you asked the Universe for," she reminded me. "Think of the poverty days. When you had no confidence or money!"

She was right. And just to underline her point, she sent me an email later, with a quote from Robert Farrar Capon, a priest, author and chef, born in the 1930s, who said:

"Older women are like ageing strudels. The crust may not be so lovely, but the filling has at last come into its own."

And it dawned on me then, that I am that strudel.

A CELEBRANT SHARES

Ten years ago, we'd never have come across this dilemma. Now it's much more common. A colleague writes:

* * *

'Does anyone have any experience/ideas for a renewal of commitment ceremony for a couple who have been together for twenty five years?

'It wouldn't normally phase me, but I'm a bit stuck, as over the last couple of years, the man has had a sex change to female.'

CHAPTER 17: FORGET ME NOT

The best bit about working with so many families is knowing you've had a real, meaningful impact on so many lives. The worst, is that by service seven hundred, I just couldn't place names or faces out of context any more.

Part of this I blame on the aforesaid menopause; (I won't dwell on this section because I don't want to alienate those who haven't experienced a bad one); but suffice to say against a backdrop of sleep deprivation, it's not a regular day if I don't lose my keys; lock myself out or delete an important document. (I won't even mention the time I went to the wrong crem or; horror of horrors; went to the correct one, but with no service notes in my folder) That was a very, very bad day.

So already battling against unforgiving natural forces, throw into the equation the stress of meeting about one hundred new people a week. This varies of course, depending on the size of the family, but it's a reasonable estimate when conducting 5–7 services a week on average.

That might sound a lot, but at £210 per service, it in no way reflects the time we spend on the whole thing. Put another way, if we break it down into thirds, the job is the visit; the writing and the delivery. Would you get a professional plumber or electrician to go on a family visit (an 'evening callout') for £70? Or could you entice a professional copywriter to produce several thousand words of script for £70? Or a professional speaker to turn up at a venue and speak and conduct an event for £70? You can see now why we have to work in 'volume' to earn a living.

Amongst the swathes of people we meet, of course some families do stand out and stay in the memory. Usually because they were particularly lovely; or awful – like the family that carried the coffin into the chapel, arguing over the top of it the whole way!

Or they can be particularly funny. I always think of the family from Castle Vale who described their youthful but streetwise mum as being, 'Like Peter Pan, but with violence.'

Or perhaps the deceased had an exceptional and memorable story; or again, maybe the circumstances were particularly tragic.

But in the main, it's face after face after face. And because we don't spend enough time together for them to become embedded in the brain, there's no recollection if someone should make contact again.

It's awfully, cringingly embarrassing.

This potential for discomfort can start right from the beginning, when I meet a family. As the meeting progresses, of course I want them to feel like they are the only people in my life. And I can hand-on-heart say they have 100% of my attention and care when I'm with them. But so does the next family.

Consequently, if the phone rings a day or so later, and somebody just says 'Hello Ruth. It's Simon Jackson', I can't automatically make the link to the person he's calling about; especially if I have a crop of people with the same first names.

Names tend to go in waves and trends, and because (as a rule) we're saying goodbye now to those born in the 1920s to the 1950s, there's a stream of men named Bill, Les, Wilf, Stan and George. For the ladies it's Alice, Hilda, Joan, Betty and Cybil. In years to come the Laurens, Emmas and Kylies will be replacing them, and their celebrants will face the same issue.

I've usually got around twelve services in preparation at any one time, all at various stages. Some are just preliminary notes. Others are written and waiting for approval. Some are approved, printed out and waiting for the actual day.

On one occasion, nine of these twelve services were for ladies called

Susan, Sarah and Sally. Three of them were married to Edwards. And four of them had daughters called Claire.

It got to the stage when I wouldn't answer the phone if I didn't recognise the number; just to be sure I wasn't going to start having a conversation about the wrong person!

That's one way of dealing with the problem from the security of my home; but when you meet people face-to-face later on, it's a totally different kettle of fish. And fate has a whole array of circumstances with which to test you.

One you couldn't invent was when I was attempting to sell my house. The minute I opened the door to the potential purchaser, she shrieked, "Ruth. It's Ruth. Oh I recognised you straight away. How are you?"

My mind whirred. She had to be a former client. Quick, quick!!! Was she connected to the gangland funeral, where half the mourners were handcuffed to prison officers? No – too nice! Think again …

Or was she from the family that brought in a Formula 1 tracksuit for the deceased to wear for his cremation; only for the FD to point out that it was flameproof, so probably not ideal for the job?

She reminded me that I'd done her partner's service a few months back, and we made the link through the house ('the new one on the corner by the traffic lights') – and then thankfully I remembered her name was Sandra. Phew – one point to me!

However, the estate agent then piped up; "And you did my father-in-law's last year."

"Oh God,' I thought, 'Here we go again.'

Sometimes I bump into people at the crem weeks later, quite by chance, when they may be there to collect their loved one's ashes. And it's all an awful blur. Whole families stand before me, expecting me to remember them. The same when I see people at someone else's service. But they're out of context by then. It's not their family I'm serving that day, and my head is full of other peoples' names.

One of the worst examples of just how overloaded I got was when I saw a familiar face at the back of the crem, just as I was about to start a service. He smiled and gave me a small wave, and I was sure he was from one of my previous families.

After the service, I went outside to the paved exit area by the gardens, to greet the mourners, and he eventually came out.

The conversation went like this:

"Hello Ruth. Great to see you. Lovely service. How are you?"

(Mind spins frantically. No name coming to mind.) "Oh I'm great thanks." (I need to make a connection quickly, so I opt for the one I now think it is). "And how are you? You know. After the loss of your dad?"

He looks at me quizzically and nods to the man next to him. "I'm fine. And I think he's OK too thanks."

I want the ground to open up at this point. "Oh God. Sorry. I've got to come clean. I thought I'd done a service for you. How do we know each other then?"

He looks visibly shocked, then says, "Ruth. We walked the dogs together, several days a week, for a year and a half!"

I'm not only mortified but crestfallen at this. Because I still can't remember him.

I finished all the hand shaking, and returned back to the car feeling dreadful, worried that Alzheimer's was setting in early, just as with my own father.

But when I later shared the story with a colleague who works at a funeral directors', she cheered me up, saying, "Don't worry love. We all do it. People come in and say 'I'm here to see mum', and we can't place them either."

She then told me how she once led a family to the entirely wrong chapel of rest. The family, who'd been sobbing uncontrollably, stopped as one when they saw it wasn't the right person.

She finished by saying, "But I don't know what was worse. I put them in the right chapel and took them coffee a bit later. They were in hysterics this time. The bloke in the flat above had come home for a lunchtime nap. He was snoring through the ceiling like a pneumatic drill!"

I felt better after hearing these stories, but still worried, I went to the doctor's for a memory test. She asked me if I'd ever had a TIA. I admitted I'd forgotten that I've had not one, but two. Not a great start.

Then she gave me a memory test, saying, "Remember Bill Smith. He lives at 54 High Street, Pershore. I'll ask you this at the end of the test."

The doctor then asked me what year we were in (2020); and who was Prime Minster (Boris Johnson). After a few more queries, she asked me to remember the man's name and address, which I did with no problems; Bill Smith, 54 High Street, Pershore.

I left the office feeling mildly cheered, but still not convinced things were 'right'.

This was confirmed when I woke at 2am, bathed in sweat, panicking that I'd missed a client off my rota. I actually ran to the office, and heart pounding, began searching frantically for the file for Bill Smith.

I knew then that my work/life balance just had to change.

A CELEBRANT SHARES

A lack of manners is something we often come up against:

* * *

'Here's a suggestion for the partner of the lady I've just seen. Why don't you switch the TV off when we're talking, not down; not subtitles ... OFF!'

Colleague reply:

'You're lucky! The most distracting thing I've had so far was a young man, sitting barefoot, picking his toenails throughout the whole meeting!'

CHAPTER 18: SPARE TIME

I decided that time out would be the answer to the exhaustion. And more laughs. We celebrants know how to have fun in our spare time: we wear bright colours; laugh out loud a lot and even eat fatty bacon against the advice of our doctors. I just needed a bit of reminding.

So, alongside the concerted effort to catch up with friends and enjoy a few nights out like normal people; came the perfect solution, in the shape of a booking for my band.

This would allow me to not only play some music and see my old friends, but also to earn a bit of money; despite the fact it all began with a rather odd call:

"Hello. Oh God. Can you help me? My mum has died and we need some music on Tuesday." (Ok – admittedly it's still death, but playing Irish/Celtic party music is always fun, regardless.)

"Oh, I'm so sorry for your loss." (Check diary). "Yes – I think I can help. What's your name?"

"Theresa. Oh God. We really need music. Can you do it? Can you? Oh God – you must think I'm mad!"

"Er no. I'm sure you're fine Theresa. You're probably just grieving. Yes, no problem, I can help you out. So what are you looking for?"

Theresa explained she wanted Fields of Athenry, (a maudlin Irish song about a woman's husband being shipped off to Australia for stealing an ear of corn to feed the bairns).

This was to be played on the violin at the graveside. It had to be timed just as her mother was lowered down. And then she wanted some music at the wake, but she didn't know how long for. And she couldn't confirm a venue yet.

So there we had it. Not particularly clear instructions, but she seemed happy with my suggestion of a duo for £550, and my proposal to play for 45 minutes as people came in, take a break during food, and then another hour for a bit of jigging and general dancing.

I put the phone down, thinking it was a fait accompli. But no! Over the weekend, Theresa phoned me five more times, with minute tweaks to the instructions. Could I start playing, the second the bearers lift up the coffin to lower it? Did I know Green Fields of France as well, because she liked that? How much money did we say again? Oh God – you must think I'm mad. No I don't, you're just grieving. Ah, well I feel it sometimes. How much money did we say again?

Alarm bells were ringing a little by now: (how often have I used that phrase in this book? I must pay more attention to my gut feelings), but when it's a funeral, you just can't let someone down. I had to work on the basis that I'd committed to being there, along with my friend Jobe, and that was that.

So we turned up at the allotted time at All Saints in Kings Heath, Birmingham, ready to play by the graveside at Mary McNamara's final farewell.

Which is all well and good, except when we arrived, it was instantly apparent that All Saints is a church set in concrete grounds. Not a blade of grass in sight. It wasn't the best start.

Luckily, there was a horse and a glass funeral carriage outside the church, and a couple of FDs standing around. I sauntered up, violin case in hand, and told them I was there to play.

They didn't look very interested, but volunteered that, 'The service is still going on in there. Running late actually.'

The lady FD nodded at the door of the church, before adding darkly, "We've had a lot of problems with this family. A lot."

She momentarily looked as if she regretted the statement, adding, "Never mind. Forget I said that."

I thanked her for the info, whilst thinking, 'Yes, that's fine. Problems or not, but it still doesn't help me. Where's the bloody graveyard?'

She suggested that perhaps Theresa had meant the crematorium grounds five miles down the road, where Mary would be taken to after the service.

She then helpfully added, "But it'll be ages yet. Why don't you pop in there for a cuppa?" She gestured to the little café next door.

At that moment, on a chilly March morning, nothing seemed more welcoming, with its steamy windows, the promise of hot coffee, and maybe even a sausage bap.

Jobe looked thrilled at the idea, so we dived in, and placed an order, rather greedily, for two all-day breakfasts.

The coffee arrived fairly quickly, but as time ticked on, there was no sign of the food. I felt the beginnings of panic rising. I was starving-hungry by now, (I literally can't function if I don't eat regularly), and a bit worried that I wouldn't be able to play.

Ten minutes, fifteen minutes passed. I joked that perhaps the all-day breakfast was actually how long it took to cook.

And then, just as the two plates finally landed on our table, the glass carriage swept past the café window, with Mary McNamara in-situ.

"Fuck. Typical!" said Jobe, grabbing his bread roll and two sausages, attempting to make a sandwich as he ran to the door.

Shamefully, I picked up the plate (and to this day I don't know why), I tried to scrape the contents into my mouth (a bit like you'd fill a waste disposal).

The egg hit my face and burnt my cheek. A sausage slid off my chin to the floor. Don't even ask about the beans. All I know is I left the café wearing more food than I'd managed to eat; although triumphantly, I did manage to construct a bacon roll.

We ran to the car park, slammed the car into action and roared off. It was very tense – but thankfully we caught up and arrived at the same time as Mary.

I tore open the violin case, and attempted to tune up. It was a disaster. My fingers were so greasy I couldn't turn the tuning pegs. Jobe was useless: hanging off a memorial bench in the background, shaking with laughter. But to his credit, he didn't allow me to go to the graveside until I'd combed the dried beans out of my hair.

So minutes later, there I am. Bean-free, fiddle tuned, mourners gathered, and Mary being carried over to the graveside. Everyone edges closer. It's very tense, and it occurs to me I haven't a clue who Theresa is yet, or her family. And I'm about to play for them all. The priest does his thing, and then nods to me.

I put the fiddle under my chin and begin. Plenty of vibrato and despite the greasy fingers, it did sound lovely. The slow, sweeping mournful notes echoed across the silence and the solemnity, out into the ether. It felt genuinely very moving. The burly Irish man to my left obviously thought so too. Lost in the music, he suddenly (and very loudly), proclaimed "Beaudiful. Fuck-in-beau-diful."

I nearly dropped my bow. But this being an Irish 'do', nobody batted an eyelid. I played on, drawing things to a haunting end, then bowed to the grave and melted into the crowd.

The next challenge was to get to the Dog and Drake before the mourners, in order to set up the full PA system. The plan was to be playing the up-tempo 'fiddly dee' music by the time they arrived.

It nearly killed us, but we managed it: puffing and panting in and out the doors; carrying heavy speakers, racing around like lunatics to set up the stage. But like the true professionals that we are, it was all done and perfect when everyone turned up.

We played for three quarters of an hour or so, and then took a break when the food came out. I still hadn't met Theresa, so I flagged down the priest as he passed.

"Excuse me father. We haven't met the family yet. Could you point out Theresa for me please?"

He gestured to the corner where a large lady was seated, surrounded by people. "That's her over there, dear. She's been let out especially for today."

Let out? What could he mean? It soon became apparent …

I walked over to Theresa, said hello, introduced Jobe and offered my condolences again. She didn't seem that interested in any of it. In fact, she was positively vacant. I gently leaned over (I hate this bit), and said that I didn't want to be insensitive, but who did I see for the money?

Theresa detached even further, and gestured to some other corner of the room, saying, "My brothers will sort it."

I asked again, "Could you show me who your brothers are then please?" (The room was full of Irish men with rotund bellies; straining shirts; rosy faces and wavy hair. I was going to need a bit more than that.)

I approached a group of them, hoping for the best. And to cut a long story short, they were having none of it.

"How much? Daylight fecking robbery!"

"And we didn't book you anyway. Theresa did. And she's mad."

It became apparent that Theresa had been sectioned a week or so prior, and had booked me without the knowledge of her family. That would explain the constant references to her saying 'You must think I'm mad'. But it didn't explain how, if they didn't want us, they'd been happy to let me play at the graveside, and for the first half of the wake.

The atmosphere became so tense there was almost a fight. And with me at 5'2" and Jobe built like an anorexic whippet, I didn't rate our chances that highly.

In the end, after *much* to-ing and fro-ing, the family went to a cashpoint and came back with a couple of hundred quid. We were paid off, and both of us were more than relieved to get away in one piece. We drove off, shaking with laughter and nerves, me thanking high heaven that was the last we'd see and hear of the McNamara family.

Or so I thought. Three weeks later, I got a call from Theresa.

"Oh – you must think I'm mad. I'm so confused, but we're doing probate now. Would you send us a receipt for the £200 please?"

I told her she'd have to see my brother about it...

* * *

Another example of crossover between my work and hobbies came in the car boot world. I genuinely love car booting, as it not only earns me a bit of money here and there, but provides ample opportunity for comedy and interaction with others. However, the first thing you need is the stock to sell.

In the lean years, before I was making a living at anything tangible, and living on a tenner a week for food; I simply asked my friends. I cleared out their lofts and garages; their garden sheds and backs of cupboards. I sold literally anything I could get my hands on: from a cracked teapot and a half-used bag of corn plasters; to a state-of-the art hearing aid.

The thrill of either finding a bargain at the sales, or selling something no longer needed never really goes, so imagine my excitement when I came upon several boxes of stock quite by chance, on a family visit.

I'd gone to see a family called the Scraggs. The FDs had prepared me somewhat in the phone call beforehand, warning "I don't think they're coping with life very well. But they're very sweet."

I turned up to meet the Scraggs at a run-down multi-storey block in the centre of Birmingham. I had low expectations, but nothing could have prepared me for the enormous pile of rubbish on the lawn outside.

Two mattresses; and a bedside cabinet with a peeling transfer of a rose on it. CD cases; swathes of tatty fabric; thousands of gaudy silk flowers; a curtain rail and so much more: all curiously topped off with a hamster cage, like a cherry on a cupcake.

My first thought was fly-tippers, but that was soon put to rest by a disgruntled group of council workers, hanging round the bins. Apparently, the Scraggs were having a clear out. They'd already choked up the rubbish chute with DVD cases, and the debris on the lawn was theirs too. "Fucking pains in the backside," one of them grumbled.

"Problem family," another agreed.

"Wipe your feet on the way out," a third laughed.

I braced myself and knocked the door. The son Gary answered, with a chirpy, "Come in! Don't mind the mess."

He then proceeded to show me around, explained they were having a clear out and how they'd 'only got seventy six more bags to go'.

And he wasn't joking. Mum Betty (the deceased) had been a bit of a hoarder. In the back room, bags were piled up in stacks, floor to ceiling. When Gary threw open the door to show me, there were no words to describe the smell; it almost whipped the lining off the back of my throat.

At first glance, the room just appeared to be bags and nothing more. But then I heard a rustle from the corner, and a face appeared behind a bag; a bit like a hamster popping up through its straw.

"You can come out now dad," encouraged Gary. "There's space if you're careful. I've made a pathway. Use the Zimmer now."

And that's how I met Eugene, who'd spent the last six weeks trapped in the room. Using a chamber pot and surviving on sandwiches that Gary had lobbed over to him (ah – that explained the smell), Eugene was more than a bit wobbly on his feet. It just hadn't been safe to move when all Betty's stuff was lying around, so he'd taken to his bed. And now, Gary had literally dug his father out.

We moved on to the living room to await Eugene's grand reveal. More boxes and bags. Tatty photos hanging at angles on mis-matched wallpaper. Bits of carpet stapled together; (70's orange swirls and green florals). A curtain pole with scraps of fabric hanging from it. Mountains of silk flowers in the corner.

Eugene crashed through the door. Hugely fat; almost immobile; in stained tracksuit bottoms and a nylon sweater. He was covered in scabs and sweating profusely. He almost fell into an armchair, wheezing as he landed. "Christ! That's as far as I'm going today."

"This is Ruth," Gary said. "She's here to talk about mam."

Eugene nodded. "Good."

Gary turned to me, very serious now. "We want her to have a good send off. Doesn't matter how much it costs. I've spent £250 on the buffet already. So it doesn't matter now does it dad?"

"No," said Eugene. Obviously, a man of few words.

I turned to try and engage him. I offered my condolences, and thought I'd break the ice by chatting about Betty and how they met. What he liked about her when he first saw her.

"Everything."

I knew from Eugene's initial greeting that he was capable of stringing a sentence together, so I persevered.

"And what about hobbies Eugene? What did she like? Did you do anything together?"

"Karaoke."

"Okay. Any particular artistes?"

That was the one. Eugene was unlocked!

"Tom Jones. Ah, she liked a bit of Tom Jones. Didn't she Gary? Oh yes – Tom Jones. Remember when we sang 'What's New Pussycat' at Butlins? On that 60s weekend? Oh she loved Tom Jones …"

Eugene faded out, resumed his glazed expression, and stared at the wall. A little tear escaped. He let it run, down his chin and into the folds of his neck. I didn't get much more from him after that.

I got a little bit from Gary about Betty's lifestyle: she was a hoarder (yes, we know that bit). And she made her own curtains every day. He gestured at this point to the rags hanging from the curtain rail. At first, I thought he was having a laugh, but he was serious. These scraps of fabric, were thrown over the rail, and 'hand sewn' every morning before work.

I felt humble, judgmental and sad. The depths of depravity that some people live in is shocking, and I was sitting in the middle of it, right then. And just as with the two brothers I'd visited in Tamworth, with the stained mattress in the middle of the room, and the wallpaper dripping with nicotine; all this family were trying to do was their best for their loved one.

And I'd do my very best for them, despite the lack of information. But before I left, I decided perhaps I could be of practical help. Just knowing there's no way they'd have a car, I offered to take a few boxes to the tip for them.

Gary seized my offer, but seemed affronted at the suggestion of going to the tip, insisting I went to the charity shop with the stuff instead.

"These are mum's ordaments," (sic) he explained. "I can't bear to see them thrown away. She worked so hard for them. Pass them on to someone who needs them."

And so I took three large boxes, down to my car, passing the swearing council workmen en-route.

"More crap?" one of them called. "At least that's a few boxes we don't have to deal with!"

I laughed as I went past. "Ha! You never know. They may contain a hidden treasure or two!"

Even as I said it, I knew it was highly unlikely, but it reminded me of when a neighbour of mine found a bracelet at a car boot sale. It turned out to be worth over a grand, so I decided then and there to take the boxes home and check before passing anything on.

I spent three hours on my knees releasing Betty's treasures from their tight newspaper bindings, but any excited anticipation soon faded. The 'ordaments' were of the kind of quality you'd see at a funfair. I didn't know whether to sling them or to open a seaside gift shop.

Amongst other things the boxes contained:

Eighteen identical cavorting miniature clowns, complete with small hoops.

Twenty seven slightly differently designed, but also identical miniature clowns, holding small dogs under their arms.

A slutty-looking mermaid lying on a rock with her tail open. She was complete with mis-matched breasts and finished in a lurid turquoise glaze.

One manic smiling teapot, with a leaf on its lid.

Two evil-looking 'lucky' pink cats with Chinese faces and grossly over-sized heads. (Who commissions these things? Who works in procurement at a factory and thinks 'Ah yes! That's what we need. A large run of lucky pink cats with over-sized heads? There's a big market for them out there!) And who is this market? People like Betty I guess!

Anyway – on we go…

One large floral pomander, and two small pomanders, all without their plastic seals.

A bell from Portugal that said 'I love you mum.'

A wooden telephone savings box with a label on that said 'Welcome To Blackpool'

There were at least fifty vases in varying degrees of garishness: some with ropes of leaves wound around them; others with sprouting fauna and flora, or perhaps a random animal or bird attached to the top. There were also literally hundreds of animal figurines. Nothing collectible like Wade, but cheap plaster or china: everything from lambs leaping and dogs on hind legs begging, through to a baby dinosaur breaking out of a plastic egg. Betty had an eclectic taste in knick-knacks that's for sure.

In the end, I compromised. I didn't send them to the tip. And I didn't send them to charity. I decided to include them on my next car boot expedition, at the local community hall.

They took two hours to re-pack, and then unwrap again on the day. And when I'd finished, my table looked like an explosion in a pound shop. I sat there for three hours, on a cold Sunday afternoon, and managed to sell one solitary leaping lamb. Apparently it was so kitsch, it was deemed by the buyer to be amusing and suitable for display. But the rest of it, as I suspected was tat.

The table cost me £8.00. I sold a lamb for £1.00. And I'd spent a total of six hours examining the stock, unpacking it, re-packing it and then unpacking it again for the 'sale'.

The rest of it went to the tip after all, but I suppose in a way I'd helped; even if it was just a bit of rubbish removal for the Scraggs.

And you know; I have to put things into perspective. For me, it was a bit of a punt. For the Scraggs, poverty and struggle was their everyday life.

This realisation was made all the more poignant on hearing the story of how, when the FD returned to deliver Betty's ashes; they arrived on the doorstep, at exactly the same time as the bailiffs …

A CELEBRANT SHARES

A kind-hearted celebrant does her bit:

* * *

'Loving the diversity of this job. I met the very distraught husband of the deceased whose funeral I'm taking next week. When I entered the house, I was greeted by three dogs.

'After a few minutes, the two big dogs attacked the tiny Chihuahua. It was a very disturbing fight. I instinctively grabbed the Chi and held him tightly on my lap the whole two hours I was there.

'His human daddy said, "This always happens. I can't look after them. I work twelve hour shifts and I can't have the dogs any more."

'So now I've come home with another funeral to write, and a dog! I'm only fostering him as I don't want a pet, but I really love him already. I have arranged for a wonderful friend to have him live with her in Wales. He will have the best life there. He will be leaving me on Wednesday, I'm going to miss him already, but I will enjoy the time I have with little Rico until then.'

*Update ... 'wonderful friend' has now changed her mind.

CHAPTER 19: IT'S GONG TIME!

Hollywood has the Golden Globes and The Oscars. Science and literature have the Nobel Prizes. Crime writing has the Gold Dagger and musical theatre has The Olivier Awards. There are more, but I'm sure you get the gist.

It took me years of to discover the industry has its own too. Imaginatively entitled 'The Good Funeral Awards', they're described by its creators as 'British eccentricity at its best: up there with the 'Best Kebab' and 'Loo of the Year Awards!''

And they're not joking! This quirky ceremony is the climax to The Ideal Death Show: the event that recognises 'outstanding service to the bereaved'.

It origins go back to 2011, to an event in Bournemouth celebrating the HBO TV series 'Six Feet Under'. And since then, it's gone on to become a real highlight of the industry calendar.

Each year, the celebrity host is someone tenuously linked to dead people. Pam St. Clement hosted one year on the basis that her character, Pat Butcher, died of pancreatic cancer on EastEnders.

In 2015 it was Ian Lavender, (Private Pike from Dad's Army), chosen by virtue of being one of the last cast members who's not dead yet. And also, in the words of the organisers, 'because someone like Julian Clary costs about £14,000.'

TV's Penny Smith also presented it a few years ago, (maybe because she's dead gorgeous?)

And now things are so popular, The Good Funeral Awards have

been dubbed the Oscars of the industry, with good reason. In fact, it's become so successful, that in 2017, five new categories were introduced in order to reflect changes in practices and attitudes.

So, as well as the usual categories for things like 'Funeral Director of The Year'; 'Celebrant of The Year'; 'Clergyman of The Year' and 'Mortuary Technician Of The Year' (the list goes on); there was a new 'What To Do With The Ashes' award, designed to showcase the great number of options available to families wishing to memorialise their loved ones' cremains.

There is now also an 'End-Of-Life Doula Of The Year Award'. Doulas (pronounced Doo-lahs) are better-known for providing support to women in childbirth, but within this context these individuals, (sometimes called 'soul midwives'), help to make the dying, and their families, feel safe and supported, as the person makes their transition from this life to whatever comes next.

When David Bowie and Anita Brookner (novelist and art historian) went for a direct cremation in 2016, this picked up on a new trend; reflecting the desire of some people to cut out the funeral service altogether. And to cover that, there's now the category of 'Best Direct Cremation Provider.'

In addition, out went the 'Embalmer Of The Year' award, replaced by a more general, 'Care Of The Deceased Award,' open to anyone in a back-room role in the care for the body.

There are also around twenty other awards, including the extremely popular, 'Gravedigger of the Year'.

My friend Amanda's husband Dave won that in 2016. That was a great year for them both, as she was president of the British Institute of Embalming at the same time. Now that's a power couple for you!

Dave even ended up going on BBC's 'The One Show' to talk about it, although it's still a trade secret as to how that category is actually judged. All he could offer when I asked him was, 'A good head for dimensions probably.'

That's fair enough. I still remember the horror of one of my funerals, a burial, where the coffin was lowered in to a very 'tight' space, and it got stuck, just like an elevator between floors. The family were hugely distressed, and I had to complete the service trying not to focus on the awfulness of it all.

I have no idea how the grounds staff solved it after we'd gone, and to be honest, sometimes it's better not to know the details.

This very subject was raised as part of an article in 'More To Death Magazine.'

In a feature entitled 'A Gut Full of Funeral Directors,' the writer said:

"My personal little grumble is the chronic problem of funeral directors failing to supply the correct coffin sizes to cemeteries, who of course want to dig the right-sized grave. What the hell is their job if not to measure and convey coffin sizes accurately? A core business activity you would have thought? Hopeless!"

One journalist who learnt a lot more detail about the industry than your average punter, wrote about her experience of attending the show on the internet site Buzzfeed.

Hayley Campbell reported: 'The average individual organises 2.4 funerals in their lifetime. However, they tend to happen decades apart so each time we go in knowing nothing. The landscape of death is always changing. I was told there is no other consumer experience on earth like buying a funeral: ninety three percent of people will drop £5,000 in the first funeral directors' joint they walk into because no one thinks about this stuff until a time when they don't want to think about this stuff'.

She also pointed out:

That within three years of being buried in a cemetery you will have – at most – two visitors a year. Within seventy years you will be forgotten, just another slab of concrete in a forest of swiftly-dilapidating concrete.

Also, that 100% of undertakers hate Andrea Bocelli. (I can second that. When you've heard 'Time To Say Goodbye' hundreds and hundreds of times, the feelings can become irrational!)

But I digress … Hayley continued:

Apparently, fat women over the age of forty decompose faster than any other demographic.

One in three hundred bodies putrefies early: a particular problem as morgue fridges aren't made to last forever.

How she also learnt that some shrouds are only fit for burial, not cremation. Apparently, it's to do with the flashback: the cremation machine is set to 750-800°C, and as you push the shrouded body in, any lingering vapour from a treated material is likely to throw flames out the door and burn the crematorium worker's eyebrows off.

It was a brilliant article, and very much tongue-in-cheek; but really touched on how many different roles and aspects there are to the industry, and the dedication of the people involved at every level.

My particular admiration is for the backroom staff, who have to deal with some very, very unpleasant scenes. You've either got the stomach for it or you haven't, and as someone who used to have to leave the school science lab when it came to anatomy and dissection, there are no prizes for guessing which category I fall into.

Even the front of house arrangers don't escape it. These lovely ladies that meet the families at the funeral homes, and make them so welcome, have to deal with it too.

A friend of mine casually dropped into conversation recently that she had to be in early for work, 'So I can sew Mr Miller's lips back together.' On questioning, she explained the family were coming in to see him that day, and the side of his mouth had sprung open. She therefore had to close them, by sewing up the skin inside his mouth, leaving no traces. Just like invisible mending; and all before her morning cuppa!

But that's just the tip of the iceberg. I've colleagues who've pieced together broken bodies; re-moulded faces, and extracted maggots, one by one with tweezers, when someone has been left too long. This can happen with repatriation from a hot country, when the journey home can take over a week. And it's nightmare if the family want to view.

A common technique here is to freeze the body, and then just before viewing, extract the maggots, fill the holes heavily with some product; (not quite Polyfilla, but similar). And the final step is to strategically light the chapel of rest with a soft pink glow.

The family would then probably have no more than an hour before they'd be asked to leave, as nature would being starting its work again. To say it's a finely-managed process would be an understatement. And that's why these people have my absolute respect.

On a lighter note: many of my colleagues, quite coincidentally, seem to be called Dave. So far on my travels I've met:

Dave The Grave: the chap mentioned earlier, who won the grave-digging award.

Microwave Dave: sadly now deceased, Microwave Dave was an officiant renowned in our area for the brevity of his services; offset by the phrase, 'Well, I'm not going to make it up if it didn't happen.'

Flaky Dave: he's the embalmer with psoriasis. He works at my friend's company and she says, "You always know when he's been in and done his shift. There's a bit of a trail …"

And finally, Dave The Wave. He does hair and make-up on the corpses. A strange career choice at first glance, but as he explained when we waited in the crematorium foyer one day, "Not so different from the last job really. I used to fill cracks in car bodies. Same technique, just different materials, and a much lighter touch!"

A CELEBRANT SHARES

This Birmingham celebrant is still dining out on her particular story.

* * *

'I normally refuse a cuppa when I'm with families, but on this occasion was absolutely parched, so I said yes to a cup of tea.

'The family were busy chatting: three generations, including mum, daughter and her baby. I'd just taken a big mouthful, when the mum said, 'Hope it's okay love. Not too weak. We ran out of the normal, so I popped a bit of Lisa's titty milk in there!"

CHAPTER 20: BACK TO THE WAKE

When it comes to the wake, to be honest I'm never really sure what to do.

It stems from the early days, when I just trotted along to one uninvited, but thinking I'd be welcome – seeing as how me and the family had developed this 'relationship' and all.

When I got to the venue, it was very subdued, and there weren't many people in total. Everyone was clumped at tables, talking quietly. So they must have heard when the chief mourner came over and asked me to leave, saying, "I'm sorry Ruth. This is close family only."

I was mortified. So now I never assume that I'm welcome unless someone stands in front of me with a gold-embossed invite, signed by every member of the family.

To be honest though, it's also a bit of a relief if I'm not asked along, as there's always a mountain of work to do, and sadly, another family to see. But sometimes, perhaps as a thank you, or maybe out of obligation, or because they like me, an invitation is issued to 'go back' with the rest of them.

This often proves more than a bit uncomfortable on a social level because apart from the immediate family, I know nobody when I get there. I once found myself at a sit-down formal reception, with a table of strangers, who were all curious about my job.

Of course, it turned into a question and answer session, with the entire table tuning in. I genuinely felt that the deceased and the family should have been the focus of the afternoon, and remember feeling acutely embarrassed.

Or sometimes the opposite happens, and I don't get to chat to anyone properly, and I'm left standing on my own like a lemon, which is even worse.

I remember Len Goodman from Strictly Come Dancing talking about accepting invites to public events. He said:

"If I go, I'm expected to dance. If I don't dance, then I'm being a miserable old sod. If I do dance, and do it well, people say, 'Oh look at him. What a show off!' If I dance, but hold back a bit, then people say, 'Oh, he's not as good as he makes out, is he?' And if I decline the invitation, then people think I'm being stand-offish, or rude. You just can't win!"

It's a bit like that with declining invites to wakes. Families can seem a bit offended if you don't go, but for the reasons above, it's easier not to.

Also, what these families don't realise, (and to be honest, why would they?), is that when I'm up to my neck in work, I could really do with going home and getting on with some writing. The sight of all those plastic folders on my desk can make me feel physically sick.

Or perhaps there's another family I could be seeing, rather than sipping tea and eating cake with a room full of strangers.

On the occasions I have gone back, a few happenings have stood out for various reasons. One of them was when I sat at a table with three strangers in the café of a garden centre.

After the inevitable grilling, I asked the lady opposite me about herself. It turned out she was married to Andrew, who was sat next to me, "Although you wouldn't know it," she said critically. "He's not got a bloody word to say to me these days. Have you love?"

Andrew grimaced apologetically. His wife then proceeded to loudly tell me (and everyone in the café), that he was, "Autistic. Undiagnosed, but definitely autistic. Finds it hard to leap into a conversation. Don't you love?"

Andrew got up from the table, puce with embarrassment, leaving me with his wife to chat as if nothing had happened. Awkward!

Another stand-out experience was when the deceased's family invited me (and the live musician), back for some refreshments. They'd booked a huge room at The Botanical Gardens in Birmingham for afternoon tea, but there were so few mourners we were just lost in the vastness of the place.

Afternoon tea came out, and we went to join the table, but were told in no uncertain terms there were 'separate arrangements' for the staff! That meant us. And so the guitarist and I found ourselves placed separately from the main event, at our own little table, feeling so conspicuous, and wishing we'd not been so polite.

So for all the above reasons. I'm still working on a refusal that doesn't cause offence, but even when I don't go back, some families still stay in touch.

One of them, a lovely family from Walsall, were really devastated by the loss of their mum. So a couple of weeks later, I got a phone call from the son, Mick, with a rather novel suggestion. He wanted me to go into a recording studio and recreate his mother's funeral so the family could find some comfort.

Personally, I can't think of anything less comforting than re-creating one of the saddest days of your life; but who am I to say no to a lovely client? So off I went, armed with the script, to see my friend Darren.

Normally Darren helps me with my website, but he also masquerades as a graphic designer; editor; musician; sound engineer and music producer. He was the man to pull this together, and so days later, I found myself in his bedroom studio, talking about Mick's mum in my best warm/solemn/comforting voice.

It needed a couple of takes: (at the time the soundproofing in the studio wasn't so good) and someone out on the estate was yelling,

'Teigan. Ger over 'ere' in the background. But the final take was adequate, and so we thought the job was done.

Darren called the next day. "Just had a thought Ruth. Do you want some shuffling and coughing for the background? And maybe a few muffled sobs?"

I thought about it for a moment. "No. You're alright Daz. Keep it simple. The family just want to hear the words."

Happily, Mick and his sister were delighted. And four weeks later, I heard from them again!

"Do you do interments Ruth?"

I confirmed I did. It's the final stage, the burial of the ashes, and every now and again, a family asks me back to do this part for them too. It's definitely the completion of a circle, and actually quite an honour that they want me involved in the last part of the journey.

I said I'd look forward to confirmation of a date, and waited to hear. Mick called a week later, but it wasn't the news I was expecting.

"I'll be honest Ruth. My sister is all for you. But I think we're going to have a minister do it. The dog collar makes it a bit more convincing!"

I let that one go with a smile, as I did with a lovely lady called Suzie, who arranged the most amazing send-off for her husband.

Suzie had organised a 'normal' family-only service at the crem in the morning; but the afternoon was a totally different kettle of fish. Full of music, tributes and stories, all compered by me, it was fitting, unique and absolutely right for a man who'd been a bon-viveur, an international traveller, an amazing presenter, speaker and all-round good guy.

I did wonder afterwards how Suzie would cope without this extraordinary man in her life, so when she asked me to be friends on Facebook, I accepted happily. It would be a chance to make sure she was okay, and drop her an encouraging few words every now and then, without being too in her face.

I needn't have worried. Facebook's pictures and posts quickly showed in no uncertain terms how Suzie blossomed; out of her husband's shadow.

She took on a part-time job which she loved. She seemed to take up residence in the local tanning parlour. She had hair extensions and lost weight. She took burlesque dancing classes; and she partied and holidayed like a teenager in Ibiza. Then she turned up one night to see my band.

I didn't have too much chance to talk to her, as we were busy playing, but to say she had a good time would be an understatement.

First, she stood at the front of the stage waving wildly. Then she disappeared into the crowd, returning with some new friends she'd made.

Suzie looked worse for wear by now; high-kicking as we sang 'Valerie' by Amy Winehouse; all the while waving her beer glass in the air.

I was very impressed with Suzie's energy and elasticity, but it all went a bit wrong when she slipped in some drink, and crashed down onto our floor monitors with a sickening thud.

The last I saw of her was as the bouncers took her away: still waving her beer glass, singing, and shouting, 'Clever girl' at me, full volume, over The Irish Rover.

So now, whenever I say in my services that we aren't designed to grieve forever: I truly believe it; spurred on by memories of Suzie – the poster girl for the most magnificent of recoveries!

A CELEBRANT SHARES

A nightmare scenario for this celebrant:

* * *

'I've just finished a huge funeral for a man in the Scouting Movement. There were cubs and scouts of all ages there, some of whom were standing by me at the lectern as the chapel was so packed.

'As I was delivering the eulogy, one little girl Scout threw up spectacularly, right by me.

'I'm a 'social vomiter' and will join in if I see, hear or smell sick. It took every ounce of willpower I possessed not to falter or gag, especially when the FD took her outside, treading her outpouring right across the carpet as he went …'

CHAPTER 21: SEE ME BEFORE YOU GO

If you knew you were dying, would you call me to make plans in advance?

Would you feel confident enough to sit with a stranger, talking about the time you're no longer here, in order to make sure those you loved were spared the heartbreak of more decisions, at a time they're feeling most vulnerable?

I've only done this twice so far, but each occasion has been such a privilege. The first time was a lovely man called Adam Waring. He'd found my website on the internet and called me out of the blue.

I wasn't quite prepared for the enormity of the call. I was shopping in Tesco's at the time; so when Adam said he'd like to plan his funeral, it didn't sink immediately.

At first, I thought he was just being super-organised for years down the line. And then it became clear. He had terminal cancer, he was approaching the final stages, and yes – he wouldn't be here next year. I remember floundering for an appropriate response. I hope I gave one.

We met about a week later at his home, where Adam also introduced me to his girlfriend Tammy, and his best friend Neil. Adam's height was the first thing that struck me. He'd obviously once been an imposing presence, and judging by the way his clothes now literally hung on him, much bigger in stature too.

Another thing that couldn't be ignored was how much younger Tammy was than Adam. But in his words, 'She's the one that's really stood by me. People can bloody-well say what they like, but Tam's held the sick bowl while I've been puking my guts up. She's cleaned me up in a way partners should never have to do.'

He reached for her hand, finishing with, "She's been on the front-line with me. Haven't you Tam?" As an ex-military man, that was Adam's way of saying they'd faced the worst together.

Neil came in then. He was a good looking man in his early forties, but right now he looked like a small child that needed a good cry and a hug. "That's a fact. Make sure you put that in the service Ruth. Without doubt, she's given him extra life." He wobbled a bit before finishing with, "We've all had an extra year of this man because of Tammy's love and care."

From there, we talked about Adam's life and where he grew up, and his love of sport; ('make sure you mention the Saturday football lads'). We covered the time he sold jewellery on the beach in France to raise enough money for a flight home. And his first marriage, ('She's a cow, but she is the mother of my kids, so we can't pretend it didn't happen'). And then his distinguished military career, and time in the probation service.

By now, it had become just like a normal client family meeting. Stories were bandied around, with plenty laughter and reminiscing. Lots of 'do you remember this? No – it wasn't like that. It was 1979 not the 80s!' type banter.

It reminded me of the scene from Gigi with Maurice Chevalier and Hermione Gingold: 'It was nine. No; it was eight. I was on time. No; you were late. Yes … I remember it well.' Different perspectives, but regardless of what's 100% accurate or not, I always feel relaxed around this point in a conversation as it means people are acting normally.

As well as the stories, I'm usually looking at the interactions: picking up on snippets, perhaps not the main themes we're on at the time, but the 'asides'; the information that can take the conversation elsewhere, or be dug into a little deeper to make an anecdote more authentic.

Like I said in the chapter about Tony and Jim in Tamworth, it's amazing the gems of information that people toss out, quite inured through familiarity as to how interesting it actually is, or what an achievement it portrays. It's part of my job to find these gems and polish them up to make a much richer, more rounded service.

One thing that did make me smile throughout all this, was Adam's insistence on thanking all the ladies who'd passed through his life. It was a fairly lengthy list, and included a few apologies for the occasions he'd not been able to take things further.

"I just want to square it all up," he said. "I don't want any questions un-answered. I want everyone to get on when the day comes, and for everything to be in order. And for my son to be proud of me."

This was particularly important to Adam, as he'd lost his first child at the age of eight. Neil confided in me later that he thought the shock of the son's death brought on the onset of the cancer, but we'll never really know. Sometimes it's just best to stay in the moment, and deal with the here and now.

I left the meeting with whole mixture of feelings, from sadness through to admiration and everything inbetween, but the over-riding one was a sense of urgency. I wanted to get as much of the service shaped up as possible, so that Adam could see and approve it.

We got as far as a draft copy before he died. We were actually due to meet again, but those last few months he'd hoped for were ultimately denied. I finished the service with Neil's input, and he was more than happy with the outcome.

And on the day? The mourners filed in to a recording of a military brass band; just as Adam had wanted. His ex-wife took up her place on the front row, (probably not as he'd have wanted), all whilst announcing herself to me as his current wife!

I saw Neil take his place, and Tammy take hers, four rows back. Still not accepted into the fold, despite all she'd done for him.

A lone bugler played to start the service, then I told all of Adam's stories and thanked his ex-girlfriends, just as he'd asked. Tributes were read, the medals were presented, and as a final gesture, a military flag was unfurled over the coffin, and The Last Post was played after the committal. It was one of the most moving events I've been involved in.

Neil rang to thank me a few days afterwards. It's always great to get personal thanks and feedback, but I couldn't help being saddened when he told me that the vultures were already circling.

Apparently, Adam's Will was being contested by the ex-wife, who didn't want Tammy to have a penny. "She's arguing over the very last teaspoon," he said sadly. "It's absolutely not what Adam would have wanted."

But at least Adam got the send-off he'd wanted: because he'd had the courage to call me in advance. And it warms my heart to know he got that peace of mind before he passed. I hope those that loved him can take comfort from knowing that too.

A CELEBRANT SHARES

Another of my stories.

* * *

'Today's funeral was a simple, straight-forward affair. Pleasant family; no major issues; nothing contentious to say or do. Perfect – what could possibly go wrong?

'I conducted the main part of the service, and then we re-convened at the graveside, where the lady would be laid to rest.

'The plot was a five minute walk away, so while the mourners waited for the coffin to be re-loaded and slowly driven to the site, I walked ahead. I got there around seven minutes before the mourners, and encountered the crematorium and grounds manager checking the grave's dimensions.

'We chatted idly for a minute or so, then out of nowhere, he began to regale me with the story of the Jamaican funeral they conducted recently, where the family asked if they could smoke a spliff and 'chill' a bit at the graveside.

'The manager said it was the end of the day, nobody was around, no more services to conduct, so he said yes.

'The family and their countless friends then all lit up, and apparently, not only the graveside but the entire cemetery was soon thick with clouds of smoke.

'After around forty minutes, the most sober of the party suddenly remembered they hadn't completed the service; there was still a box of doves waiting to be released over the grave. Symbolic of a soul flying to freedom, the idea was a lovely one, but nobody had accounted for the effect of the smoke on the poor birds.

'Five were released. One hit the fug, immediately blacked out and plummeted to the ground. One circled wildly for a few seconds and whizzed into a tree, where it stayed, glazed and panting, for two whole days. Three flew off, one returned home the next day, and the final two were eventually traced to Leicester – thirty miles away as the stoned dove flies!

'By the time he'd finished telling me the story I was biting my cheeks, almost weeping with laughter. The hearse rounded the corner, I contained myself just in time to complete the service, and the mourners were none-the-wiser.'

CHAPTER 22: NAME THAT TUNE♫

In most services, there's music to come in to, music to leave to and very often a piece for 'quiet reflection' in the middle of a service.

Over the years, there are certain trends that we hear over and over again. These include the following:

Time To Say Goodbye (Andrea Bocelli & Sarah Brightman)
We'll Meet Again (Vera Lynn)
Always Look On The Bright Side of Life (Monty Python)
My Way (Frank Sinatra)
Softly As I Leave You (Matt Monro)
Look For Me In Rainbows (Vicky Brown)
Jealous of The Angels (Donna McTaggart)
Supermarket Flowers (Ed Sheeran)
A Thousand Years (Christina Perri)
Thank You For Being A Friend (Andrew Goldman)
Bat Out Of Hell (Meatloaf)
Who Wants To Live Forever? (Queen)
Dancing In Heaven (Dani and Lizzy).

Those are the classics, the ones you hear multiple times a day. But every now and again, someone throws in a curved ball to raise a smile. For example: one man, Cyril, had a wife who was a continual nagger. It was acknowledged that Vera never shut up. And that she was the boss. In fact, I included the words, 'Cyril wore the trousers, but Vera told him what pair to put on', and that got a great laugh, because everyone knew exactly what she was like.

So when it came to the end of her service, Cyril had carefully orchestrated it for maximum impact:

I finished the Lord's Prayer and then after my closing words, Cyril strolled over to the coffin, leaned casually on it with one hand and said, "Ta ta Vera. I've got the last word now."

That was my cue to press the button, and seconds later, out belted the opening bars of the song, 'Shut Uppa Your Face'!

Fortunately, everyone saw the funny side.

Another family thought it would be lovely to send off their seventy five year old mum to the strains of 'I Wanna Have Sex On The Beach!'

Sometimes attempts to change the atmosphere are equally cringe-worthy: maybe where the family want people to sing along to the chorus. Or clap hands, which generally falls very flat.

On the flipside, some of the music chosen is so incredibly sad, it's almost as if the family want to make things worse.

If there is a particularly moving piece chosen, then I make a point of listening to it many times beforehand, in an effort to de-sensitise. I can't tell you how many times I've had to listen to Benedictus from The Armed Man by Karl Jenkins. That haunting cello cuts me to the core.

But perhaps the musical moment that will stay with me forever was during a service for an alcoholic lady; (sorry, I've got to use that word on this occasion).

Her sons were in their late twenties, and had very few good memories except for when they were small, back when she was extremely beautiful, before the alcohol stole her away.

They remembered being around seven or eight, sitting in her bedroom, watching her put on make-up and jewellery before she went out for the night. So, to honour this, and bring back the rare good times, instead of music for quiet reflection they simply walked to the front with her jewellery box, wound it up and let it play.

I watched the little ballet dancer on the box twirl along to 'Music of The Night' from The Phantom of The Opera. And as I stole a glance at the boys' stricken faces, it took everything I had to focus, reminding myself yet again that 'this is not my grief'.

But that's the thing about music; it's so evocative. And that's why people choose songs as reminders: usually of falling in love; first dances; baby's arrival and anniversaries. In short – special times.

Normally I'm aware of the music in a service: but when a family substituted in the song 'More Than A Feeling' by Boston, without telling me, it knocked me for six, because it was a reminder of such a special event; but sadly the event wasn't mine.

I'd just done the eulogy and announced the song for reflection. I was just beginning to take my seat, when the opening notes blasted through the chapel. My knees almost gave way, as I was immediately transported back to 1976; aged fourteen, standing in the kitchen of my best friend, Kate Abrahams' home.

In my mind's eye, I could almost feel the warmth of the sun as it filtered through the leaded window, casting shadows over the dark kitchen shelves, crammed with ornaments and cookbooks. And I could still see her mum in the corner, frying eggs, as the smell of fresh coffee wafted through.

The music played on, and I remembered that Kate and I were arguing about whether The Osmonds or The Bay City Rollers were the 'best', when in strode her brother David; home early from his work as a chef.

He was the spitting image of David Cassidy. Tall, with dark wavy hair, blue eyes and a chiselled chin. Wearing faded denim jeans and a white cap-sleeved t-shirt, he was every teenage girl's fantasy.

The sight of him whipped my breath away, because I'd been secretly and deeply in love with him for years. It's not in my nature to be closed or to hide anything, so that 'love' almost killed me at the time.

I recall David looking strangely excited as he came in. For a moment, I'd allowed myself to hope, that perhaps, it might be me? (I was wearing my best red top with the zips across the boobs), so who knew?

But seconds later, my world crumbled.

I remember Dave coughing loudly as he swept his eyes around the room, garnering attention for his big announcement. And then, against the backdrop of 'More Than A Feeling' playing on the radio, he broke the news of his surprise engagement to Lene, a Dutch girl he'd met weeks ago on holiday.

As everyone erupted into spontaneous congratulations, I remember my heart felt as if it would shatter with the pain. I'd hardly been able to breathe. I recall breaking away from the family and rushing out into the street for air. Eventually I made it home, where I must have sobbed for the rest of the day.

Based on a magical hour spent with David listening to his Rory Gallagher LPs, and fuelled by stories of 'true love' in Jackie magazine, I'd invested over two years in hoping and dreaming about us, and how the future could be. And all this was ignited, from hearing the song again.

As the final bars melted into the background, I was jolted back into the crem chapel, trembling with the residue of overwhelming sadness for the 14 year old me. And glancing over at the family, I could see they were having their own experience – equally traumatic. But I was the one that had to compose myself; it was okay for them to cry.

I wasn't to know it back in 1976, but my heart would be broken many, many times after that. Some of these would be small fissures; but other occasions, I'd be rendered almost immobile by the pain. I'd be ill through love; and later, cut to the core by infidelity. I'd be lied to, and subsequently fixed through the clarity of my counsellor, and the warm embrace of Prozac.

Somehow, I'd always recover; but I still wonder what it must be like for some of the people I meet. To love so deeply and, more importantly, genuinely. How do you recover when you've woven a dynasty together, over 40 or 50 years, and then it's gone?

It seems the loss would be unbearable. And sometimes that's proven when a loved one follows on quickly.

Science talks about 'stress induced cardiomyopathy', a temporary condition that crops up after a period of intense stress, causing the heart to enlarge. It's also dubbed 'broken heart syndrome', and I encountered it first-hand at the start of 2020.

Originally for a man called Giles, my booking suddenly became a double tribute when his wife Sonia passed away two days later.

It was such a shock. After Giles' death, Sonia had been doing well apparently. The family reported she'd rallied, put on her lipstick, and made an appointment to see the funeral director the next day. When they went to collect her, she was still in the same clothes from the day before, sitting in front of the television. Just gone.

It was the same with the death of Carrie Fisher, then just a day later her mother Debbie Reynolds' passing.

Many of my colleagues report the same experience. A brother dies, followed by his sister. Children followed by a parent; or husbands and wives who can't live without each other. If not in a matter of days, it's often just weeks apart.

I've never found that kind of love. In a way I'm glad. I don't think I could stand the pain. But thinking about it as I write, it prompts me to check Facebook and do a bit of 'light' stalking.

It appears that forty four years on, David and Lene are still happily married, with a beautiful, adult daughter. A real, genuine love story.

I imagine, in due course, they may be one of those couples.

A CELEBRANT SHARES

This subject often crops up, as Bella from Devon explains:

* * *

'A lady came up to me after a funeral today and said how lovely it had been, which was truly appreciated.

'She then told me that she is a registrar and doesn't get paid nearly as much as me. I wanted to say that I really do understand that she has a difficult job that isn't very well paid, when it should be.

'I also wanted to say that today is my birthday, I can't take the day off because I need to work, (this was the first of two funerals today). I also wanted to tell her I'd be working way into the evening and that I worked last weekend and I will be working again this weekend.

'I also wanted to say that I can only take a maximum of three weeks' holiday this year as any more would be too detrimental to my income because we don't get holiday pay, sick pay or a pension. But of course I said none of this ...'

.

CHAPTER 23: AND THEN THE WORLD CHANGED

Nobody could have anticipated the arrival of COVID 19. It certainly wasn't the ending to the book that I was hoping for, but to not at least acknowledge it wouldn't be an honest appraisal of how the industry has been affected. The virus changed life for millions of us, and death too: at least in the way we were able to say goodbye.

At first, things were sketchy. There was talk of 'trooping on'. It was no worse than the flu according to many. And people ignored the guidelines, and sunbathed in parks, and shopped and went about their day as normal.

Then came a mild form of lockdown. Schools closed, people began working from home and the instructions were to only go out if it was essential.

This is where things changed in the industry. A funeral is essential, but by handling bodies, and conducting the services, we were all putting each other at risk.

Numbers became limited at crematoriums, fifteen mourners was reduced to ten, then down to six. We could no longer meet families to hear their stories: everything was done on the phone, email and Facetime. It felt as if they were being sold short.

And the limited numbers in crems began to pose problems for families. When there are large numbers of siblings, how do you decide who gets to attend and say goodbye? It was utterly heart-breaking, hearing of families drawing straws to solve the dilemma.

And the content of the service. There was no point in providing a eulogy, parroting it back to six people who know what you're going to say. I had to become creative, to focus more on the spiritual legacy someone had left behind. Perhaps what people had learnt from them; what they'd take forward into their own lives; propped up with a few details from their life story as evidence.

It felt strange at first, but in a weird way, began to work well. As I pointed out to the families, in a way, this was more personal. All element of 'show' had been removed from the service, and this was now a simple gathering of family love, where people could really be themselves, without the eyes of others upon them.

But what never felt right at any stage, was the fact we couldn't hug families at their worst times. Or each other. The whole thing felt dreadful, and unsatisfying and exhausting. And the services kept coming, and coming, landsliding as the numbers grew.

It was during the crisis that I passed the thousandth service milestone.

All those names and different circumstances, from the poor little mites who never even got a shot at life to the quiet private men to the selfless mothers; the jailbirds; party people; the pub dwellers; philan-thropists; time wasters; devoted partners and wonderful friends.

And my final thought from seeing all this? I don't know when the crisis will end, (we are coming out of lockdown three in the UK as this book nears completion). And I don't know if we'll ever see anything like it again: but regardless of the future, my two main learnings from this privilege of a job are that:

Grief does get better. It honestly does. We are designed to repair. We wouldn't have survived as a species if this wasn't the case.

Mothers would never go on to have babies after losing a child; and people would never find partners after severe heartbreak.

Hang in there …

Life is for living, and living well. What is the point otherwise? This realisation prompted me to make some serious changes of my own.

To adjust my workload to manageable proportions; to invest in my own health; and to dare to fall in love again.

'He' turned up just as I was giving up. A widower himself, with so much love to share, what better pairing? With our shared knowledge of loss, and the fragility of life, it's time for us both to live fully again.

And I'd implore everyone reading this to do the same. To really make the most of the time you have left; because one of the saddest things I hear when I speak to families is, 'Isn't it a shame that he never did x, y, z.'

If it's a case of, 'Isn't it a shame he never got to meet his first grand-child,' then yes. Absolutely. But there was nothing that could have been done about that.

However, if it's a case that somebody has the time, or health, energy, resources or encouragement to do something, and they still don't; then it's more than a shame – it's practically a crime!

So go for it! Give us celebrants something to celebrate for you; something substantial to talk about. Don't leave us floundering, wondering how to make a service from 'She liked ironing'.

When the world opens up again, go climb your mountains; learn that language; write your book, and overcome your phobias. Tell that special person you love them. Don't let time or money or fear hold you back. Go do what your soul tells you to do. Live your life to the full. And I promise, when your time comes; we *will* find the words.

Because one day; we will all be stories …

I BRING THE WORDS (BY H. WALKER; CELEBRANT) (2017)

I bring the words for the departed and the dead
I bring the words to say who he was, what he did,
and what he said
I bring the words
with dignity, to signify their worth
words to describe a space in time, a human lifetime from birth
I bring the words
I talk of times when life was new
reflected in hearts and minds
stories to keep the memories alive
I bring the words
I place them in order, in ways that matter,
to shattered lives, when someone dies
I bring the words
I give them time, words bathed in warmth and laughter,
words to hold onto forever after
I bring the words
spirituality for the bereaved, bereft
humility, humanity, a non-religious Christianity
I bring the words when there is no-one to mourn,
no-one to hear of a past glorified, no life sanctified
I bring the words when there are no words,
no words to heal, no words to feel we make a difference
I bring the words for everyone

the rich, the poor, the old, the young
words that don't differentiate, dying doesn't differentiate
I bring the words to end the journey
to say farewell, to bid goodnight
I bring the words for life's finale,
the words for the closing of the light.

RESOURCES

This is just a small section of resources. By investigating some of these websites, it'll take you through to more and more links, and within those, you'll find everything you need.

For talking about death; bringing it out into the open and helping to make it part of life:

Death Café Network: www.deathcafe.com
Drink tea, eat cake and chat openly. There are cafes all over the world. Each café is hosted, so you'll never wander in and feel on your own. It's not morbid – it's more about being social, accepting our own mortality and helping people get the most out of life.

Dying Matters: www.dyingmatters.org
I've mentioned this charity several times within the body of the book. They're about creating an open culture that talks about death, dying and bereavement. This is a treasure-trove of information.

For one week a year, Dying Matters promote events all over the country. And for the rest of the year, they relentlessly campaign and support others seeking a fundamental change in society in which dying, death and bereavement will be seen and accepted as the natural part of everybody's life cycle.

They have an amazing resources section where you simply type in your postcode, and up come all the local organisations near you.

There's also a national section, covering anything from anxiety to bereavement support, nursing care, elderly charities, Macmillan nursing advice, help with pets when you're ill, therapists, funeral advice and so much more.

The Conversation Project: www.theconversationproject.org
What kind of care do you want if you become seriously ill? And do you know what your loved ones' wishes would be? The Conversation Project encourages people to get talking around the kitchen table: not the intensive care unit.

Final Fling: www.finalfling.com
Encouraging people to embrace life and accept death, then 'sort your paperwork, make plans, leave instructions, tell your story. And save your loved ones the trouble and stress.'

Good Life, Good Death, Good Grief: www.goodlifedeathgrief.org.uk
They work in Scotland to promote more openness around death and dying.

* * *

For information prior to death; dealing with death more naturally when it happens, and being more involved in the process on a personal level:

The Good Funeral Guild: www.goodfuneralguild.co.uk
An excellent resource aimed at helping people select reputable suppliers across the industry.

Home Funeral Network: www.homefuneralnetwork.org.uk
Great advice on the legalities and practicalities of a home-based, family-led funeral. Or simply being more involved in the process, even if others are doing the arrangements.

It's also an excellent resource for celebrants, soul midwives, undertakers, death doulas etc.

The Natural Death Centre: www.naturaldeath.org.uk
An organisation that's passionate about sharing knowledge, dispelling myths, and empowering everyone who wants to have the best experience possible when it comes to making arrangements for a funeral.

They also publish the 'More To Death' magazine. Available on subscription or viewable online via www.issuu.com

The Good Funeral Guide: www.goodfuneralguide.co.uk
The UK's only not-for-profit independent information resource.

* * *

Support whilst dealing with serious illness or preparing for death:

What Matters Now: www.whatmattersnow.org
A free and incredibly simple to do website page that allows the patient (or family) to give updates, (rather than constantly having to repeat the same information). It also allows family and friends to respond, send wishes and support.

* * *

Bereavement Counselling Organisations:

Compassionate Friends: www.compassionatefriends.org
Now based abroad but some good information and resources online.

Cruse Bereavement Care: www.cruse.org.uk
This charity provides free care to all bereaved people, as well as offering information, support and training services to those who are looking after them.

Grief Encounter: www.griefencounter.org.uk
Grief Encounter helps children who have suffered the death of a parent or sibling. It aims to professionally care and respond to the needs of each service user with an individual approach.

Sands: www.sands.org.uk
A stillbirth and neonatal death charity that works with professionals and the bereaved on everything from research to counselling.

* * *

Natural Burial Grounds:

You can find more information on UK natural burial grounds from The Natural Death Centre www.naturaldeathcentre.org

* * *

Death Doulas:

Living Well, Dying Well : www.lwdwtraining.uk
Doing Death Differently : www.doingdeathdifferently.com

Printed in Great Britain
by Amazon